2,00
Media Marketing Tricks

The Best Tips, Advice, and
Practices to Grow Your Business:
Facebook, Instagram, YouTube,
and More

By

Invictus Media

Contents

Introduction

Social media has taken over the world; gone are the days of door-to-door selling, big billboards or directories. If you are a business in this new social media age, your biggest task is, of course, to find customers. Earlier, businesses had to go out of their way to find and inform customers about their products. This was not just tiring and ineffective in most cases – most importantly, it cost far too much money. Businesses a decade ago used to have specific advertising money that they would keep aside, which would eventually eat up into their profits.

Well, social media has completely solved that problem. In this new age, you don't have to find customers in the real world as everyone is now connected in a virtual space where almost all daily interactions take place. This virtual space has become a savior for businesses because now it's easier to find customers, you can interact directly with them, and you can also study their likes and dislikes to sell products to them. Social media is free so you don't even have to spend money to advertise.

This doesn't mean that you don't have to work hard to market your business. With the advent of social media, the field of marketing has become open to everyone;

hence, it has become extremely competitive. If you want your product to stand out, you must build a brand through social media and you must stand out. Social media has immense potential to take your business to the next level, but that can only happen if you know what you're doing.

That's where this book comes in. The purpose of this book is not just to give you the basics of how social media marketing works, but to also familiarize you with different tips and tricks so that you can take your business to the next level. We are going to study different social media platforms, such as Facebook, YouTube, Instagram, etc. and look at different ways of finding marketing success on these platforms.

Chapter One

Facebook

It is no secret that Facebook is the most popular social networking website in the world. Facebook is not just meant for individuals, but also companies looking to promote their businesses on a worldwide scale.

Founded in 2004, Facebook was originally launched to help people keep in touch with each other. Over the years, Facebook managed to evolve into an advertising tool for companies, and now plays host to several businesses that use it as a platform to promote their business. Facebook for business is now not just a fad, but a very lucrative concept that more and more companies are identifying with, and incorporating, to avail multiple benefits.

Why is Facebook Marketing Important?

Facebook is the new way to market your products. If you correctly tap into the potential that Facebook has, then you will be able to successfully market your products. Facebook marketing is based on trying to capture the imagination of your audience in new and interesting ways. If you can get your audience to relate to your products, then you'll be able to sell it to them.

If you have an established audience, then you can use Facebook to influence people to create a positive attitude towards your products. A lot of companies are using this strategy; they hire social media managers - people who are exceptional at handling social media platforms to create a positive image for the product and increase its reach. You can do all of this by yourself and all you must do is understand how important Facebook is, set up your page correctly, and understand how advertising works.

Facebook is especially important for small businesses. These businesses do not have a lot of money that they can invest in expensive advertisement campaigns. They can use Facebook to create a fan-following for their products. You can use Facebook to create awareness about your products and to get to that level where you can afford those expensive advertisement campaigns.

Number of Users

Facebook is the biggest social media platform available for any marketer. It has over four hundred million active users and these are people who actively use their accounts daily. If you advertise correctly, then you can reach out to a lot of these people. You can advertise your product to them and make them aware of your product.

Customer Interaction

Customer Interaction is important because it generates customer loyalty. A customer would always prefer a business that adds a personal touch. The reason for this is simple; every customer wants what is best for him. The business that treats him better and with kindness is the one that he would be attracted towards. On Facebook, through posts and comments, you can directly connect with your customers. It's impossible to connect with each person directly in real life. That is why Facebook is so important as you can reply to each comment and take all their queries. You can show to your customer that you care about them and their needs.

It further creates more customers for you. If a business gives a personal touch to whatever they are doing, then a customer will always prefer that business. This is because the customer would feel like the business cares about him. A lot of big companies can't connect with each one of their customers directly. These customers feel like they are not being heard and they are not being taken care of; hence, it's important for them to feel like they matter to your business, and Facebook is the perfect way to do this.

Search Engine Optimization (SEO)

SEO is important for any business, as it is a way to get your business famous on Google. If you have a Facebook page, then it will show up first when someone Google's the name of your business. If you do not have a Facebook page, then it might be difficult for any person to find information about your business. Facebook links are the ones that come up on top whenever you Google something. That's why Facebook pages are significant.

Free Promotion

Facebook is simply free promotion. If people like your page, then your content shows up on their newsfeed. If they comment on your post or share your status, then it further promotes other people to like your page and they get to know more about your business. This is a free way of promotion and you don't have to do anything at all for this. This might not be very effective, and it might take a lot of time to build a huge fan following but, even if it helps you to get a couple of loyal customers, then that's more than enough. You didn't have to spend any money and yet you got a few customers.

Your page might just go viral as well. If your posts are interesting and you use interactive stuff like memes, puns, etc. to promote your page, then people will get more interested. They will share stuff like this and this will get you an even bigger fan- following. Free promotion is important for any small business and if you work hard for it, you will get some benefit out of it.

Responding to Problems

You can respond to problems quickly if you are on Facebook. If there is an issue, then you can make a post about it and inform your customers; this helps you to tackle problems in an easy manner. It further helps you to respond to problems of your customers because if a customer has a problem, he can always message you on Facebook and you can quickly solve their problems. It's difficult for a business to be available at all times, but when you're on Facebook you are always available. Even if you can't solve the problem now, at least the customer can directly connect with you.

Beating Your Competition

The best way to get an edge over your competition is with the help of Facebook. It's a competitive market out there and everyone is trying to do better than their competition. Now, Facebook might just be the edge that you need to beat your competition.

If your competition is on Facebook and you are not, then you are already two steps behind. Facebook can be the difference between you and your competition, which is why Facebook is so important.

There is a lot of competition in the food industry and almost every restaurant out there has a Facebook page. People even decide where they want to go based on the reviews that they see on the Facebook page of a restaurant. This can be the deciding factor for a customer who is confused between you and your competition. You must make sure that you capitalize on this opportunity by having a Facebook presence and by keeping your page active as well.

Customized Newsfeed

People won't see the posts on your page on their newsfeed just because they have liked your page. Facebook has various ways to determine what posts appear on a person's newsfeed. More than anything else, the thing that determines a post on their newsfeed is a person's interest. If a person has an interest in something, then all the related things about that interest will show up on their newsfeed first, so, if a person is a huge fan of food and has liked a lot of Facebook pages related to food, they will see posts by restaurants they have liked on their newsfeed.

You can use this to your advantage by posting content that matches the interests of a person. If a person has liked your page, then they obviously have an interest in your business, so try and post content that is related to your business but, at the same time, is interesting enough to hold a person's attention.

This gives you a great opportunity to get into people's newsfeeds. You can use this Facebook algorithm to make your page even more famous by posting relevant and interesting content.

Facebook also shows things that are more famous first; even under this the posts that match your interests and that your friends have liked are shown first. Posting engaging content becomes very important as the more likes and shares you get, the better the chances are of a person seeing your posts in their newsfeed. You should try out your posts on a specific group of people to see how engaging it is, as this will help in ensuring the long-term viability of your Facebook page.

You must work on your Facebook analytics; try to see what kind of content gets your audience interested, and work on your future content based on these analytics. Always remember who your target audience is so that you can customize your content on that basis.

Social Reputation

Social reputation is not about how many likes you have or how active your user base is, it is simply about having a presence on social media. The businesses that are not on Facebook are at an inherent loss because they will never be able to market their products or services as well as their competitors.

Social reputation is simply about having a page; if you don't have a Facebook page, then you will never have a social reputation. Now, the consequences of not having a social reputation stems from user behavior. A consumer will always prefer those businesses that he believes are legitimate and who work hard to gain customers. You can get this legitimacy by being on Facebook as many users tend to just search up the name of a business on Facebook to determine if they want to add themselves to your consumer base.

If you are not on Facebook, then there is a sizeable amount of people that might not even take your business seriously and, when they don't take your business seriously, you'll never become a reputed seller for them.

Facebook Apps

Facebook is also available on mobile apps. You can download the app from the app store and start using it like you would use any other app. The user interface is extremely friendly and will help you navigate through the different aspects of a typical page. Most people prefer to check the newsfeed that is available to them on their home page and remain updated with the various developments.

Facebook has various applications that can be useful for anyone running a social media business portfolio. These applications were made for the sole reason of helping businesses have a good social media presence.

Facebook Groups is one such application. You can create a Facebook group for your product, business or just your staff. The main purpose of this application is to manage groups easily; it can be slightly difficult to manage multiple groups. You can review all the posts and deal with the members; you don't have to open your Facebook app every time for this. Further, you can sort out the notifications for groups because groups tend to spam a lot; this way, you can keep your Facebook ID and group-related business separate.

The second app is called Facebook Page Manager; it's a must for anyone trying to increase the reach of their page. Managing a page is not simple and requires a lot of work; it can be hard to deal with page-related stuff on the regular app. Page Manager has a brilliant and easy-to-use interface that is perfect for anyone managing a page from their phone. It allows you to customize your page, deal with the settings and other issues just from your phone; you can work on the go with the help of this app.

Chapter Two

Facebook Page

Facebook bases all its interaction on two things — profiles and pages. A profile basically introduces a person, whereas a page introduces a company or business. A profile is created for an individual looking to represent himself or herself on Facebook, whereas a page is created by an individual to represent his or her company or business. The same individual can create an individual profile for himself, as well as a page for his or her company.

A profile can add friends (other people who use Facebook, once added, they will appear in your list of friends). These friends can be friends, family members and acquaintances of the person. The page, on the other hand, can have likes and followers. Likes refer to the number of people who like the page, and in turn, the company in question. These can be known or unknown people as it is impossible to know who have liked a page.

A profile's activity generally shows up in the newsfeed as compared to a page's feed. A person must visit a page to know what is happening on a page's feed.

There is also the option to create a group on Facebook. A group basically is a place where like-minded people can join in to collaborate. A person can create a group and invite others to join in. It can be a closed or public group depending on the creator's preference, but it is not possible for a business to own a Facebook group, they have to create a Business page for it. A business profile can partake in a group if necessary. We'll talk about groups in detail later in the book.

Setting up a Facebook Page

The very first step is to create a page. To do this, log onto Facebook.com and click on the 'create a page' button at the bottom. It will be easy if you already have a Facebook account as you can easily create a page by signing into your existing account, or you can enter Facebook.com/pages and create a page. Next, you must understand the different terms and conditions listed.

Once done, you can enter the name of the page. Remember to take your time and not rush the decision. It is best to consult with friends and family before coming up with a name for the page. Facebook allows just one change of name once the page has been created.

Once done, you can click on the type of business you

own. You will have to choose one from the following options:

- Local business or place

- Company, organization or institution

- Brand or product

- Artist, band or public figure

- Entertainment (promotion)

- Cause or community

Once you choose the appropriate option, you can move to the next step of the process. Next, you can fill in the 'About' info details before adding your website's address. Once done, Facebook will give you your unique URL for your page.

Next, you can choose the preferred page audience. If you have content for people above 18 years of age, then you must specify it to your audience. If in case you are not yet ready with your page, then go to the settings and edit the page's visibility and choose "un-publish page" to continue editing the page without being disturbed.

Here are the different page elements you can choose:

Settings

- Page visibility - here you can choose who can view your page. If you are keen on making it a private page, then you can modify the settings and make it a closed group.

- Posting visibility - here you can choose who can post on your page. Sometimes, it's important to limit the posts so that you don't end up with a page consisting of a million posts.

- Targeting and privacy for posts - this is to capture an audience. It is important to aim the posts to a certain audience, so you send the message across to the right audience.

- Messages - the messages that your page can receive. If you are taking orders from people through your Facebook profile, then you can create filters to keep the spam at bay.

- Tagging ability - people who can tag your page.

- Country restrictions - people from specific countries that can view your page. Sometimes, it's best to limit the page to only those countries where your business operates so you don't receive spam.

- Age restrictions - people of specific age groups can view your page.

- Page moderation - this allows you to prevent certain words from appearing on your page, thereby staving off spamming.

- Profanity filter - this is to prevent people from using profane words.

- Delete a page – you can delete a page if you don't like it and start from scratch.

- Category - pick a category for your company. This is quite important as people will find it easy to look for you.

- Name - the name of your company.

- Start information - you can mention the details of when your company started.

- Short description - you can provide a short description of your company.

- Long description - a detailed description of what your company is all about.

- Company overview - you can provide an overview of your company.

- Mission - you can mention your company's

mission.

- When founded - the date when your company was founded.

- Awards - any awards have come your company's way.

- Phone number - your company's phone number.

- Website - your company's website.

Once you fill in the above details, your page will be ready to roll.

Facebook Page Standards

Profile Picture

Here are the specifications for the profile picture:

- The picture must be square.

- It must be at least 180 x 180 pixels.

- It should display at least 160 x 160 pixels on a computer.

- It should display at least 140 x 140 pixels on

smartphones.

- It should be 50 x 50 pixels on feature phones.

- You must leave a space around it, so that the picture does not go all the way to the edge.

- It is best for companies and businesses to use the company logo.

Cover Photo

For the cover picture:

- It is recommended to use 851 x 315 pixels, RGB, and JPG picture that is less than 100 kb.

- You can use the graph provided by Facebook to crop the image to the right size. It is best to use a picture that is easy on the eyes and not too overwhelming.

Calls-to-Actions (CTAs)

- Remember that it is extremely important for you to guide your audience and tell them what to do on your page. Many people assume that people, by themselves, understand whatever they are supposed to do on a page; however, it pays to give them a clear instruction about the same.

- It is best to create a "call-to-action" button that will allow your audience to take appropriate action. You must also expressly mention it in words to drive across the message.

Facebook Posts

Here are the specifications for Facebook posts:

- The newsfeed images should be 472 x 394 pixels, and have an actual ratio of 236 x 197 pixels and the image should be 504 x 504 pixels.

If you need help with this specification, then here are some tools that you can use to edit the picture - Picmonkey.com and Canva.com.

Posting to Page

- Post links - you can post unique links to your page by adding them to the page.

- You can pick a picture of your choice and then post it on the page.

- You can also schedule your posts and post them at regular intervals.

- You can edit the picture by hitting the edit button. You will have a glimpse of how others are seeing it.

- If you do edit it, you can copy the new link and paste it in the box.

- It is best to check all your work before posting it as you can avoid having to delete it later.

- It is convenient to post multiple pictures at once.

- You can also add a short description to each post.

- You can easily tag people in your pictures.

- You can use the # to look for someone who has been tagged.

- You can also tag posts the same way and look for them using the #.

Additional Things to Do on Pages

- When you upload a picture or a video, you have the option of adding your location, but it will pay to exercise a little precaution and post location only if necessary.

- The video you wish to upload should be of a certain size. You can check the limitation of the video before uploading it.

- You will be notified once your photos and videos have been uploaded.

- Remember, videos will not automatically upload the audio and you must add it separately.

- For the event milestones tab, you can check the drop-down options and choose the options that suit your requirements.

- You can use the milestones option to check about the company, its various posts and the different people who can post on it.

- You can control the various tabs by clicking the "manage tabs" option and edit it to your liking.

- One important point to note while posting on a company page is to log out as the admin and log into your personal profile before making a comment. If you have hired someone to manage the page then they can be instructed to reply through the account or create another one.

- Remember, it is extremely important to share your business page on your personal timeline as it helps with capturing a bigger audience. After all, the main motive behind creating a page is to gather as big a crowd as possible, so it is important to advertise it as extensively as possible to be noticed by as many people as possible.

- Remember that your page is synonymous with your company and vice versa. You must maintain a professional tone while posting on the page and instruct the person managing your social media pages about the same too.

Best Practices for Viral Facebook Posts

Facebook is fundamentally based on posts and their ability to go 'viral,' which means that your post must be so encapsulating that it draws people in. Here are some tips and tricks for viral Facebook posts:

Use Emotions

Facebook is not about selling products, it's about actually connecting to people. You can't connect to people unless what you sell to people are emotions. It doesn't really matter what your product is on Facebook if you want people to care about your page and your brand; you must emotionally connect with people.

The only way that you can connect to people is by relating the utility of your product with things that make people relate to it so, if you're trying to sell say clothes, you can't just show people what you're selling and hope that they wear it. Instead, if you put up a story of how your clothes are made, and the people that work endlessly to ensure that the clothes you make are perfect, you're far more likely to gain public attention.

Don't Overdo It

Of course, trying to connect with your potential audience is important, but make sure that you're not trying too hard. If you continue to latch on to every new trend and keep on making jokes, it's eventually going to saturate your audience. Also, many brands think that they can connect to the younger generation by using their slang and style but try not to partake in silly things like this. It's only going to make your posts seem fake as if you're trying to just be relatable for the sake of it.

It's important to remember that you're selling something at the end of the day. If you're going to try your hardest to make it seem otherwise, it's only going to make your audience unreactive to what you have to say.

3. Keep Posts Short and Specific

The one key role in Facebook marketing is to keep your customer's attention. If your customer sees posts that are too long and if all your posts are videos, they're not going to engage a lot.

Be direct with your audience and tell them what you're selling while, at the same time, trying to connect with them. Most brands tend to have far more success with shorter posts than they do with huge advertisement campaigns. If you do decide to make longer posts, just remember to add pictures and paragraphs. This will at least make your audience interested enough to continue reading.

Keys for Running a Facebook Page

When it comes to setting up a killer page on Facebook, it is important to make it as interesting for your audience as possible. You must put in the effort to make it look professional to help your audience connect with it in a better manner.

Here are some Facebook page strategies that you can

employ to make it entertaining for your audience:

Personality

It is quite important for you to add in a certain personality to your Facebook page. People should be drawn into it and feel the urge to 'like' or comment on the page. If you settle for something mediocre, then it will not work in your favor. A good idea is to hire professionals who are good at molding pages and making them interesting for the audience. You must instruct them to review the audience and prepare an analysis of their general characters. Doing so helps in preparing a fitting schedule that will make your page popular. You can also look at the strategies that some of the other companies are employing and come up with a plan that is in keeping with the same; however, it is best to maintain a little originality and remain true to your company's policies.

It pays to have a good sense of who you are and what your company stands for. If you, yourself, remain confused, then it will go against you. It is best to work out an image that you would like to portray and then pursue the same. Remember that things can look like one thing in your mind and another thing on paper so it is best to create a page and check if it looks exactly like you planned it.

Consistency

Remember that consistency is key. You must be consistent with your posts and they should be coherent. Your Facebook page should be a slice of your store and the products you sell there. Don't make it too different as it can confuse your customers. If you have a team working for you, then instruct them to post the posts at regular intervals and not keep the audience waiting. A good trick is to know when people prefer an update to come their way and give it to them, but don't make it boring, as you must keep your audiences engaged. Again, you can look at a successful company's strategy and come up with a posting schedule that suits your own company. As mentioned earlier, it is best to aim for the early evening slot, as that's when most people are active on Facebook.

Frequency

When it comes to maintaining an online profile for your company, it is extremely important to be as frequent as possible. You must try to post new posts at regular intervals so that people know what to expect and when to expect them. A golden rule is to post in the evenings, as that is when most people expect new posts. Try to increase the frequency of the posts as and when the company grows. Some companies prefer to post new posts three times a day as that helps in keeping the audience glued, but it is important not to get carried away and post too many things all at once. Don't overload the audience with too much information, as it will end up confusing them. Keep the information relevant and coherent. You can always do a short trial and error to see what is working for you and what isn't. For example, you can ask your audience how often they would like to receive a Facebook post from you.

If they are happy with the frequency, then you can maintain or change it according to their preference.

Business Goals

It is quite important to be in sync with your business goals and update your page from time to time by keeping in mind the main motives. Your page should be a thorough representation of your company's motives. Your page should speak of your ambitions. It should portray your true intentions. It pays to incorporate a little of your company's policies in every new post.

Converting Your Profile to a Business Page

If you already have a Facebook profile and wish to convert it into a page without creating a separate one, then you can do so with much ease. Here is an instructional for the same — go to

Facebookpage.com, and search for 'convert my Facebook page,' and there you will be able to automatically convert your current profile into a page.

Here is how you can merge your profile with your page:

Click settings and download a copy of your Facebook page. Pick the profile to page migration option. Remember; once it is merged, you won't be able to retrieve your profile. You must make up your mind before making the transition. To merge your business page, go to settings, choose the general tab and choose between the merge pages and merge duplicate pages and choose pages that you want to merge. Remember though, that the two pages must be identical; including the same exact address and information; otherwise, they will not merge into one.

It is easier to start from scratch and create a page dedicated to your company; however, you might have to fill in all the different details from scratch.

"Page-Only" Strategies

When it comes to promoting your Facebook page and using it the right way, it is best to adopt "page-only" strategies to enhance its appeal. This means that you run exclusive offers on your Facebook page and not have them elsewhere.

Here are some Facebook-only strategies that you can employ:

Merchandise

It is a good idea to start with the merchandise. This includes offering exclusive goods that are not available at the store. For example, you can offer a whole product that people can only buy through your Facebook page or website and not at the store. Alternately, you can offer a customized product that is exclusively available online. Say, for example, you offer to customize a product to the customer's liking by changing the color scheme or encrypting a message etc. You can also offer a product in a color scheme or pattern that is different from whatever is available in store. You must make it obvious by making appropriate announcements and tell your customers they are online exclusives. You can also tell the people in your store to check it out online to divert their attention to your "page."

Offers

You can run exclusive online offers. These can include schemes such as 'Buy One, Get One Free' or get a complimentary gift free etc. Such offers are sure to generate interest and enhance your page's value. Again, it is important to advertise it, so people are made aware of the offer. You can send out emails detailing the same and tell people about the offers you have carved out for your online audience. You can also advertise it in your store or hand out flyers to people, so they visit your Facebook page.

Rewards

You can reward people who bring in 'likes.' This works well as people will be prompted to bring in more and more people to 'like' your page. The reward needs to be a little appealing to capture your audience's interest. You can offer coupons, free merchandise or specially designed merchandise. All of these will prove to be quite appealing and help lure in more people to 'like' your page. You can make the announcement on the page and also on your other social media accounts. You can also mention it on your website and inform the people who visit your physical store.

Discount Coupons

You can offer discount coupons and discounts to your customers. These coupons will allow them a discount on the products and services that you have on offer in your store. They will be able to avail these coupons only on the Facebook page. Again, you must announce it on all your social media accounts, such as Twitter and Instagram, to inform people about the same.

Contests

Contests are a fun way to get people to visit your page. It helps people get involved in a better way. You can announce about the contest on your Facebook page. The contest can be related to the products or the services that you offer. It can be something like adding a tagline or completing a phrase or posting pictures of the products. You must also announce a good prize that will excite people enough to partake in the contest. Setting a short deadline is a must, as you will have the chance to increase your page views in a short period of time.

Events

You can also announce events on pages. These can be events where people meet up and get to know each other better. Such events will also help you know your audience better. You can organize food and drinks as well.

Events can help you out a lot if they are done correctly. All you must do is create an interesting event, invite as many people as you can and spread awareness with the help of your page, so try to promote your business and product with the help of an event. The benefit that you get from this is that you don't have to spend a ton of money sponsoring events organized by other people; a lot of people sponsor local events to get name recognition.

You can use Facebook to get name recognition without spending a lot of money through events. Events can get famous if they are publicized in the right way. Firstly, identify the kind of event that your target audience would be interested in and, once you have done that, start inviting people and spread the word about the event.

Say you are a local bakery who wants name recognition in your locality. Start by thinking of a creative event that you can use to publicize your bakery and, at the same time, giving your customers a fun time. Create a related event on Facebook and start inviting people that you know are in your locality; use your contacts as well as your Facebook page. Use the event to promote your bakery and keep publicizing your bakery so that your small business gets name recognition.

This is just the start. By spending a little more money, you can create events that will attract thousands of people. Start slowly with events that you don't have to invest a lot in, and once you see that the events are helping you in streamlining revenue, you can start expanding to bigger events to get even more name recognition.

These are just some of the different offers you can run online and you are not limited to just these. You can modify them to suit your company's policies.

Apps for Business Marketing

There are various apps that every Facebook marketer must have to be more successful. These apps are not officially made by Facebook but are meant to help you in running a business page on Facebook.

These apps are straightforward but, at the same time, they will help you to manage your page even better. They will help you with the content on your page and even with tracking progress. They are a must-have for anyone who is running the Facebook page for a business.

Custom Tab Apps

These are the kind of apps that help you to install a small website on your Facebook page. You can have customized videos, images and what-not on a single tab with the help of these apps. These apps are helpful because not everybody has brilliant editing skills and computer skills. If you are one of those people, then these apps will do everything for you so that you can give your customers everything that they might need.

Recommendations: Hayo and Tabsite.

Email Capture Apps

These are the apps that will help you to capture the email addresses of your Facebook audience without disturbing them. It can be really difficult to get email addresses out of people, and you need these email addresses because it expands your reach. You can get the email address from the people who visit your page by making them click on certain links; hence, you don't have to ask for email addresses directly. Recommendations: Constant Contact and AWeber.

Quiz and Poll Apps

These are the kind of apps that help in preparing polls and surveys to post on your page. Quizzes and polls are an important way to gain customer feedback; the more customer feedback you have, the better you can serve your customers. You need apps for this purpose because it's difficult to get people interested in taking a short survey or quiz. Quiz and Poll apps ensure that whatever you create is viable enough to attract people easily. Recommendations: Woobox and Antavo.

Automatic Posting Apps

These are the apps that can be a savior for anyone who does not have the time to regularly update the Facebook page of their business. Automatic Posting is something that is available on Facebook, wherein you can create a post now, and then schedule when you want that post to appear. The post will be on your page automatically at the time that you set. This is helpful because not everyone has the time to regularly post stuff on their page and, if you don't post stuff, your page starts to look dead. This gives a very bad impression to any customer who visits the page. Scheduled posting ensures that your page seems active even when you are too busy to post anything. This can be done directly on Facebook itself, or there are apps that will do it for you. Recommendations: Buffer and Rignite.

Social Media Integration Apps

Social media integration is the concept of being able to use different social media sites with the help of just one app. By using these apps, you can connect different social media sites to your Facebook page, so that whatever you post on other social media sites also appears on your Facebook page. If you post something on your Twitter or your Instagram, it will automatically be posted on your Facebook page with the help of

Social Media Integration apps. You get a lot of benefit out of this because many users follow a couple of social media sites exclusively, and these users might just get connected with you on other social media platforms if they see your Facebook posts. Recommendations: Pagemodo and Tabsite.

Contest Apps

Contest apps help you to organize contests on your Facebook page to increase participation in your business and keep your audience interested. Contests can be difficult to organize and take a lot of strength, but you can deal with all of this with the help of Contest apps because they make it easier for you to organize a contest, and they make sure that you comply with the terms and conditions of Facebook. Recommendations: Offerpop and Votigo.

Chapter Three

Facebook Ads

In the previous chapter, we looked at Facebook pages in detail. In this one, we look at Facebook ads. Ads are what companies use to advertise their products or services on Facebook. As mentioned earlier, it is quite important for companies to put out information about their products so more people are made aware of it.

These Facebook ads are mostly displayed on the right-hand corner, but you can choose where to place them on the page. You can do so by changing the settings.

You can read on the subject by accessing the "Facebook ads guide." You will have the chance to educate yourself about the "Types of Ads" that can be created. Here are some of the choices you will find:

- Click to website - this will take you directly to the destined site.

- Review design recommendations - you can review the designs that can be incorporated in the ads.

- Carousel - the carousel will help your audience view multiple products and services at once.

- You can add in tracking to see how many leads you have captured.

- It is important to leave behind a "call-to-action" option that your audience can click on to take appropriate action.

There is a big difference between the ads that play on the website and the ones on the app. You must customize the ads to fit well with the app. Here are the steps you should take:

- You must first install the app and have a clear idea of what ads will look like on it.

- Next, you must see how engaged your audience will be.

- You need to be aware of the local events and happenings to appeal to your audience.

- You should keep track of other company's offers and try to compete with them as much as possible.

- Remember that it is important to distinguish between your website views and mobile views.

You can make use of a video testing tool to check the ads before they go live.

Basics of Facebook Advertising

Facebook advertising is a very powerful tool that you can use to promote your products and services. Advertising on Facebook is very easy once you know how to go about the process. Here is how you can get started with it:

Once you have your ad permit, go to the "manage your ads" button on Facebook.com/adsmanage.

Once there, pick the options you would like to incorporate in your ads feature. If you wish to create an ad from scratch, then here are the steps to follow:

- Choose the type of ad that you wish to control. This depends on what you want the ad to stand for.

- Next, choose the objective of your campaign and incorporate it in the ad as extensively as possible.

- Next, choose the demographic that the ad will be displayed to. Doing so will help your ad connect better with the chosen audience.

- Next, decide on the budget that you wish to allot for the ad. It pays to have a number in mind as it helps you stay on track and prevents overspending. You can set the budget based on how big you want the ad to be.

- Next, you must create an audience for your ads. You should keep in mind the audience that will be viewing your ads and incorporate elements that will please them.

Creating a Page 'Like Ad'

When it comes to creating a Facebook ad, you must follow a few steps to make your Facebook ad relevant to your audience.

- You can start by creating the ad.

- Remember that it is quite important to promote your Facebook page so that more and more people have the chance to view your ads.

- Just like a page, it's important to set a budget for your video ads. If you don't set a budget, then you run the risk of over-shooting it

- It is important to pick the right demographics to show the ads to make a big impact. If you create an ad that does not appeal to the chosen demographic, then it will end up being just a wasteful campaign.

- It is important to choose the right campaign name for your ad as it will greatly help in capturing your audience's attention.

- You must make use of thoughtful pictures that work well with your chosen audience.

Creating Audiences

It is no secret that your ads will not work if you don't create an appropriate audience for it. Here is what you can do:

- You can click on the audience tab to choose the right audience for your work.

- You can customize the audience that you already know and pick out people who suit your campaign the best.

- You can choose where your audience comes from. For example, it can be from your friend list or from your Facebook Page.

- You can upload a list of people, import them or pick out specific people from your list of people.

- Next, you should agree to the terms that Facebook puts forth.

- It is best to name your audience so that you know what they comprise of, for example, if it is a group of teenagers, then you can name it "teens."

- It is a good idea to test your ad with a dummy audience to see if it clicks with them.

- Once you create the ad, you can import your audience over.

- You can upload appropriate images to suit your ad campaign.

- You can choose how long the ad will run for on Facebook.

- Remember that all the ads go through a screening process, so it is best to preview the ad before going live with it.

- It is extremely important to create an audience for all your ads.

- You can save a target group and name it to create specific ads for them.

- The target groups will be chosen based on demographics.

- You can avail a graph that will show you the size of the demographics.

- It is best to try the ad out on an audience just to

make sure that it is driving across the right message.

Facebook Ads

- Click on the create ads tab.

- Choose the objective of the ad.

- Add in the name of the campaign.

- You can either choose an audience or create one from scratch. You can also import an audience from your page.

- It is vital to add demographics to capture the right audience.

- You can pick the options to add in multiple images or a single image.

- You can always connect to your Facebook page.

- You can click on the languages tab to pick the language of choice.

- It is extremely important to add in a CTA to help people take the right course of action.

- You can generate a conversation tracker to keep

tab of your conversations.

- You must create a pixel.

- It is best to name your ad campaign to facilitate future reference.

- You should keep track of the page views.

- Make a note of the URL.

- You must validate the ad that you create.

- You can edit your ad by clicking on the "campaigns" tab.

- You can use an old ad to serve as a base for another ad by changing up the images.

- You can keep the basic concept of the ad intact and work on the images used.

Video Ads

Video ads are much better than picture ads as they will capture your audience's attention in a better way. Here are the steps that you can adopt to create video ads:

- Start by creating a plan for the ad.

- Next, choose your target audience, just as you would for your regular ads. You will have to choose the right demographics for your video ads.

- Next, you must choose the budget for the ad. As is with regular ads, it is best to set aside a budget, as it will help you stay on course.

- You should upload a video that has the specifications of 720p, and a ratio of 16 x 9.

- You must preview the ad before going live so that you can make any changes to it if you think it is important to do so.

Reports

It is quite important to look at reports in order to understand how your ads are faring. Here is how you can do so — start by clicking on the "reports" tab present on the left-hand side, and there, you will find the following options:

- General metrics.

- Choose demographics to look at.

- Export as excel file.

- You can pick the cost per click option to see how much you are making through the clicks on your ads.

- You can filter the results to see what is working well for you and what is not.

- If you have hired a team to investigate the analytics, then you can add people if you want them to have access to the account and make the desired changes.

- You can avail an email notification if you want to be notified for the clicks.

- You can always access the account history to peek into the history of your account.

Remember, it is quite important for you to treat your Facebook page as a primary tool to communicate with your audience and update them about the company's latest developments. Do not get carried away and post things that are of a personal nature. It is also best to not get into a tiff with any of the customers posting on the page. You can hire a team to answer the different customer queries and try to post new content as frequently as possible.

It is important to keep up with the enthusiasm and not allow the page to go cold.

Chapter Four

Facebook Groups and

Analytics

In this chapter, we will look at how you can use three important features of Facebook – groups, analytics and Facebook Live to help your business succeed.

Working with Facebook Groups

Groups are great for marketing, especially from a business point of view because they allow you to interact with a highly targeted audience. People join groups only if they have a specific need, and they expect people in that group to fulfill that need. With groups, you can increase your awareness about what your customers want while, at the same time, directly advertising your business to them.

How to Join a Group?

Groups are just small communities on Facebook and

you can join over 6,000 of them. If you want to join a group, click on the Groups tab on your Facebook profile and you'll be redirected to the Discover Groups page. On this page, you can search for different groups based on keywords, or find groups based on the pages you've liked or the interests that Facebook is aware you have.

For a business, the best thing to do is to just type the name of the kind of business that you do. If you sell clothes, then just type clothes and you'll find multiple groups where people just want clothes recommendations or discussions. Some groups are public while others are private. If it's a closed group, you will have to send a join request that will then have to be approved by an admin. You can click on the description of a group to find out the rules of engagement in that group. It's better to follow these rules; otherwise, you might get kicked out.

Creating Your Own Group

If you're a business, the best thing that you can do is create a community around your product. This way, you'll be able to directly talk to your customers and make sure that these customers are engaging with what you're saying. Unlike pages, groups are far more engaging, and you will have active customers who will care about what you're selling.

You can create a group by clicking on the Groups tab on the left-hand side of your profile. You'll have to give your group a name first – make sure that this name is catchy. After that, add a few friends of yours for now to start the group. Set your group up by adding a cover photo that will entice the audience. Now, what you need is an audience, so, for now, you can add some of your friends that you know who will be interested in your products.

If you want to get more people in your group, you can do a few things. You can promote your group on your website and Facebook page and, if this doesn't work, get access to email subscription lists for the field of business you're in and mail the group invite to potential customers.

Facebook Analytics

Facebook is a platform that has a diverse number of users and each user has a different way of interacting with your page and your brand. Facebook Analytics help you to market your products better by giving you detailed information about potential customers who follow your page. With this information, you can create targeted posts and learn about the kind of interaction that is popular with your audience.

To start, go to your Facebook business page and click on Insight. The three sections that you will see now tell you three important things about your page – the number of people who liked your page in the last week, people who saw your posts, and people who 'engaged' with your content. Engagement means liking, sharing or commenting on what you have posted.

The page 'likes' are great for your business because it not only tells you about how many followers you're gaining, but also explains where you're getting likes from, so you'll get to know if people like your page because of your posts or because of a Facebook ad. If you want to specifically find out the contribution of an ad campaign on the number of 'likes' you got, you can just click or drag on a specific time.

The next section is the post reach section and it is a most important one. This section will show you how many people saw your posts, and how many of them interacted with it by liking, sharing or commenting. This way, you can find out what kind of posts creates more engagement with your audience, and you can isolate the reasons for it to continue making posts like that.

Benefits of UsingFacebook as a Social Media Marketing tool

Facebook allows businesses to start conversations with their customers. It provides the ideal outlet for companies to reach out to and generate a rapport with their customers, be it new customers or old ones.

It is vital for all companies to receive feedback for their products and also marketing campaigns. It helps to know whether the audience is satisfied or are looking for something different. It also gives companies an insight into customer expectations and throws light on their buying patterns. This helps to market products the right way.

Facebook lets customers post their opinions on the brand's page. This enables the brand to know exactly what the customers are looking for and can attract other users' attention.

Facebook pages can prove to be a good lead generation tool for your website. The more customers your page collects, the bigger your website's traffic. Your Facebook page can also end up appearing on top of the results page in Google.

Facebook can be used to increase the potential audience for your product and therefore put you in a better position than before to sell it.

Whenever a person likes your page, it will be displayed on the person's timeline therefore increasing the potential of your page going viral and find new customers.

Using Facebook Live

Addressing Comments

One good way of using Facebook Live video for your business is to start a debate on a topic your customers have been requesting. For example, if you have launched a new product then you can have a live video to address your customers' questions.

Now you may think that it is easier to simply go about answering their questions in the comments section, but, having a live streaming session can help you answer all the common questions at once without having to refer to a previous comment several times.

This will make the audience press play for the live video session, as they will be looking forward to hearing the answers you have to give. If some have missed the live session and ask the same questions, then simply share a replay of the live video.

Giving Customers Insight

Facebook live can be used to give your customers an inside look of your business and how things operate. Say, some of your customers would like to know what goes behind the scenes on a daily basis; you can activate the live option to show them your day-to-day working. Not only can it be educative but it is also your chance to show your customers how you work hard to deliver the final product to them.

Promotions

Facebook live can be used to promote an upcoming event by creating posts about it to tell your fans that it is coming up by making a special announcement. You can share details about the event on the live video. When you wish to announce the event, tell them that you will be having a live video session about the event and post a URL that they can click on to be redirected to the live session.

Use Bitly to create the URL so that it is easy to track it and can be shared on all of your different social media platforms. The live option can also be used to share live footage of you attending conferences and meetings and sharing it with your audience.

Teasing Your Audience

Facebook live can be used as a tool to tease your audience about a new product. It can be used to give them a sneak peek of the product. For example, if you have just created a new product or received it then do a live video to share the details of the product with your customers. You can add links in the description or comment section to let your customers pre-order the product, as that will generate a sense of excitement among them.

Answering FAQs

As you know, it is important for all businesses to have an efficient customer service platform. Answering questions will help you connect with your audience in a better way. If you have launched a new product and there are tons of questions coming up, then go through them and pick out the ones that need the most attention. Have a live session to answer all the questions in one go. You will always have the video ready to be used in response to any further questions that the audience might have on the topic. It can be used as an archive and customers redirected to it whenever they come up with the questions.

Engaging with Facebook Group Members

If you have a Facebook group for your business that is exclusive to members who have purchased from you, then you can have special live videos that only they can access. It can be about product demos or announcing new events etc. It can also be used to announce a meet up of existing customers and getting them to bring in new ones.

As you can see, Facebook live can be used to grow your business and attract a larger audience base.

Chapter Five

YouTube

YouTube marketing is quite different from any other kind of marketing because it's entirely dependent on videos. You also must dedicate far more time and energy into creating content, which your subscribers will want to watch. It might be easy to get people to like a Facebook post and engage with it, but making them watch your videos and follow your business is another ball game.

Setting Up a YouTube Channel

Regardless of your purpose for creating a YouTube channel, it doesn't take time to create one. After your channel has been created and approved, you can change its appearance, edit your videos if necessary and perhaps group your videos into different playlists. Whether you are creating your YouTube account for your business or just want to start a personal brand, here is a simple 3-step checklist you can follow:

Step One: Create a Google Account

This is important provided you didn't have one previously. By default, your YouTube username will be your Google username; hence, when you upload your videos, this username is what everyone else sees; however, you are free to change it once you're on YouTube. If you have a Gmail account, you have a Google account, and you have access to all Google products, such as Google Play, Google Drive and YouTube but, before you can sign onto YouTube from your Google account, you will be asked to provide your first and last name. This is the name that will be used to identify you on YouTube; hence, you can either choose between different names or choose your actual first and last name.

The name of your YouTube channel, as you know, is very important. I would say the popular YouTubers are split almost equally between using their real name and a brand name. Now, this really depends on your preference for privacy and what your channel content is going to be about. For example, most vlogging channels tend to use their full name, whereas most gaming channels tend to use a brand or made up name. Be creative.

If your channel is going to be about an idea, concept or a brand channel, then you're going to want to use the brand name. Coming up with a brand name is something you should think about long and hard. A few tips that you can mix and match:

Alliteration e.g. "Charisma on Command"

- Wordplay/ Rhyming e.g. "PewDiePie"

- Try a single word e.g. "Vsauce"

That being said, your channel name isn't overly important as long as the content is quality. For example, most cannot even pronounce the channel name "Kurzgesagt"; however, their videos consistently pull in millions of views. Pick a name you like and are passionate about, and stick with it. Once you have filled these required fields, select "Create Channel."

Step Two: Customize the Appearance of Your Channel

This is important since the first impression of your channel is extremely important. Of course, the quality of your videos is supreme above all the rest; however, the truth is that it is best to cover all your bases.

Some of the most important things that you should change are:

- The channel's description

- The channel's art

- The channel's icon

If you want to change these basic things, head on over to your channels, and you'll see a button called 'edit' next to whatever needs to be changed – just click on it.

Channel Description

This part of your channel is important. Although the amount of people that check your channel description in relation to your subscribers is going to be fairly low, it's good to include links to any other social media profiles that you want to share and links to your website. Many YouTubers also include here an FAQ for questions you might be asked a lot. A crucial thing, if needed, is to include a business email here. Don't use your personal email. This can be extremely useful for increasing the revenue you make on YouTube, and we'll go into detail on this later in the book.

You can also add a featured channels section, and add a trailer to your channel. A channel trailer is important, as it lets people know what they can expect on your YouTube channel. What I would do here is feature my most popular/best video in order to get the greatest early impression of my channel possible. You can also change how the videos are laid out and also enable 'channel comments' under the discussion section. Any change you desire to make can be done by clicking the settings icon (it is next to your subscribe button), and then enable the "customize the layout of your channel" option.

Channel Art

As mentioned previously, you can get a nice banner made for as low as $5 on Fiverr, and you can also use a free stock photo from pexels.com or use any wallpaper you like. This is not such an important part of your channel, but you can perhaps use this to advertise a book you've released, or have a link to your website there.

Channel Icon

This can be an interesting photo of yourself, a professional photo, or even taken on an iPhone. The main purpose of this photo is to draw people to click on your channel, so try and make it eye-catching. A scientifically-based trick is to include your face in the icon (if appropriate) and pull a face that's related to your YouTube channel (check out Vsauce's icon) or just a picture of you smiling.

You can also use your channel name as inspiration for the logo. If you're really stuck, you can even go on the website Fiverr.com and get a logo made for as little as $5, and they're very good quality. You can also get your pictures professionally edited to include your logo on them here. People also opt for drawn versions of themselves, and this can be really good, especially if you're not the most photogenic (like me).

Step Three: Start Uploading Your Videos

To get access to the upload page, first, you have to log in and then press the 'upload' button. You can find this button on the right-top side of the YouTube site. When you want to upload your videos, you can either:Drag videos to the upload page,

- Click the large upload area to browse for videos from your PC, or

- Press the 'import' button, which you will find next to the 'import videos' side, to the right of the upload screen. With this, you can upload photos from even Google photos.

Another option that you can use is to make a photo slideshow for YouTube. It is available on the right-hand side of the upload page.

Pro tip: Make sure you select either public, unlisted, private or scheduled as it suits you when you want to upload videos from your PC. When you make your videos public, anyone can see them. When they are unlisted, only those that have the direct link can access the video. When they are private, only you can see it and you have to be logged in before you can see them. When you want to schedule your videos, you can set the time when they will be available to the public.

Other Factors You Need to Keep in Mind:

If your web browser is up-to-date, the video you want to upload should have a maximum size of 128 GB; otherwise, you will only be able to upload a video with a maximum size of 20 GB. Your video editing software should give you a good idea of how big your video is before you render it, but, most of the time it's rare you'll be exceeding 20 GB.

- Unless you verify your YouTube account, your videos cannot exceed 15 minutes in length. Once you have verified your YouTube account, this limit is removed. This is good to keep in mind depending on the type of content you want to make.

- Make sure your videos are in mp4 format when you want to upload them. If not, you will get an "invalid file format" error; however, you can convert your video to an acceptable format, and I would recommend Adobe Premiere or Sony Vegas Pro for this purpose. These are paid software, of which a free alternative is Windows Movie Maker (I would, however, not recommend this solution).

- You can use YouTube's video editor to add titles, captions, split the video into clips, add photos and make video transitions. More on exactly how to edit your video later.

If you want to easily manage your videos, put them into custom playlists.

Chapter Six

YouTube Channel

Before you crank up your camera and start blasting videos into the universe, take some time and think about why you're creating a YouTube channel and what your goals are. Building a channel can be a long, hard, uphill trudge and if you are completely focused on numbers and analytics, it can be disheartening at times. (If your goal is just to make some quick cash through pre-roll ads, I can assure you that there are much easier and faster ways to make money online.)

- Why do you want to create a YouTube channel?

- Showcase your creativity?

- Make money?

- Make friends?

- Build a brand?

- Market your business?

- Tell a story?

- Promote a product?

- Showcase your work and get a job?

- Increase traffic to your blog or website?

YouTube is an amazing platform for all of these things and all of them are legitimate reasons to start a channel.

If you aren't really into video games, don't start a video game channel just because PewDiePie is the biggest channel on YouTube right now.

For a great example of someone who has built a huge audience for a very niche passion, check out The Blu Collection. This channel is all about a guy's toy collection with a huge focus on toys based on the Cars movies. At the time of writing this, he has over 1 billion views and is adding almost 2,000 subscribers a day. I've only skimmed his channel, but he obviously loves what he is doing and this has translated into a thriving audience.

The vast majority of shows on YouTube are created without even thinking about the potential audience. You can still find success, but taking some time to think about your audience in advance can give your project an extra edge.

Ask yourself honestly:

- Will anybody really want to watch this show?

- If your answer is yes, who are they?

- Why are they going to watch?

- What is the best way to communicate with them?

- How are they going to find your show?

- How are you going to connect with them?

Ultimately, I think there is an audience for just about everything but, by thinking hard about who your audience is, you will be able to design a show that resonates with them more immediately and you will find them faster.

When it comes to YouTube channels, it's better to not use the term audience; instead, try to use the word community. Audience implies a one-way communication. Community involves not only two-way communication, but also something more complex. This is one of the things that really differentiate web shows and television shows, so don't make the mistake of being a narcissistic person. Cultivate your community and treat your viewers with respect.

If you're a super creative person, you're probably going to want to re-invent the wheel on a regular basis but, trust me you don't have time to do that. To build a loyal YouTube following, you need to produce videos on a consistent schedule – the more consistent, the better. I've tested just about every conceivable variation of upload schedule and frequency. Based on this testing, the most important factor seems to be consistency.

If you're doing something that is relatively simple from a production standpoint, I highly recommend designing a show that you can produce weekly. If you're producing something more ambitious, such as short films or animation, a consistent schedule is still important. If you can only produce one episode per month, determine a monthly schedule and stick with it.

Lots of people get hung up on all the equipment they think they need to get started. The truth is that you probably already have everything you need to at least get started. The camera quality on most smartphones is good enough for you to start. There are very popular vlogs that are shot with webcams. Instead of over-thinking it, figure out how you can make the most out of what you've got. This applies to your content as well. Build your show around locations, props, talent and the resources you have easy access to.

Your regular viewers (the foundation of your community) are not showing up every week to see your fancy camerawork, and many times they're not even there for the topic of the video. They're showing up to see (and connect with) your on-camera personality. Design your format so that it spotlights and reflects your on-camera personality.

Best Practices for YouTube Videos

Over the past few years, some major production companies have launched big-budget productions on YouTube. We saw a lot of these when YouTube was doling out millions to fund original content. Many of them have taken a traditional television approach to the style. Big budgets, amazing videography, aggressive editing and even some mid-list "stars" have characterized these productions. There were a few successes, but the majority of them failed. In my opinion, they failed because they were just making "TV" for YouTube rather than recognizing the unique opportunities offered by the platform.

In theatre, there is the concept of a "fourth wall." This would be the invisible fourth wall in front of a customary three-walled box set. This is how the audience "looks" into the world of the play. When an actor acknowledges the existence of the audience, it's referred to as "breaking the fourth wall." This concept exists in the world of film and television as well. In YouTube, the fourth wall is pretty much always broken. The most popular YouTube personalities talk directly to their audience. Some of the biggest recent scripted hits have come from Pemberley Digital (Lizzie Bennet Diaries) who have built their entire company on a broken fourth wall. They've now produced several incredibly successful stories that all are essentially characters talking into a webcam.

When watching videos on YouTube, there is always the sense that a person made the video or at least liked a video enough to upload it. Your viewers want a sense of connection and relationship with you. Embrace this, rather than obscuring it with fancy editing or flashy graphics that will look outdated next year.

There is no perfect format for a video. There is no ideal length. There is no magic bullet that works every time for every video. The only way to get close is to get started, pay attention to the response (analytics) and then make tweaks to improve what you're doing. That being said, here are a few tips to use as a starting point:

Format

OPENING: A quick introduction that tells a person exactly what they are going to see in the video. For food videos, make sure to get a shot of the finished dish in the first 10 seconds. Ideally, end it with a joke, or something that is a good lead-in to the intro music.

TITLE/INTRO: An introductory sequence with some music and the title - just try to evoke the overall feel for the show. Keep it short - 7 seconds or less.

THE MEAT: Time has really been of the essence in everything up to this point, but now we can slow down and get into the video itself. The pacing is determined by the subject matter. Towards the end of this section, use annotations and a spoken CTA to ask the viewer to subscribe or recommend another video they might be interested in. I'd rather have them jump to another one of our videos than go searching for something else.

END CARD: This end card continues the branding that we established in the title/intro, but has at least one CTA, if not several. If someone has made it this far into the video, they are either already invested in your show, or very interested. This is a great chance to give them something to do next. Send them to another one of your videos, or to the main website. Once you've launched a few videos, you can go to Video Retention in Analytics and see how things are working.

See if you can pinpoint when people are bailing on your video. If people are bouncing off at the very beginning, it may be time to go back to square one; however, if you get a big drop-off at 4:30, take a look and see what's happening in your videos. We will discuss analytics in detail later on in the book.

Gear

If you're going to produce a show, you're going to need a little bit of equipment. It's really easy to get hung up on this point and spend endless hours on camera websites and forums doing "research." Cameras are so good right now and camera technology is evolving so quickly that you really are just wasting time. By the time your camera arrives, something new and better will be announced.

Find something that works for you and your project and start shooting. What you need will depend on what kind of show you're going to make. Conversely, if you don't have a budget, what kind of show you make will depend on the gear you have.

If you have an iPhone, you could invest in a few inexpensive accessories and apps and shoot high-quality footage. A new phone from Samsung even shoots 4K video.

At a bare minimum, here are the things you will need:

Camera

The release of the Canon 5D MKII started a revolution that completely blurred the line between video cameras and still cameras. Some of the best video quality is coming from DSLR cameras.

Image quality is, of course, incredibly important, but audio quality is even more important. You've got to have a way to plug a microphone into your camera. You could sync the sound from an external recorder later, but that adds time in post-production. For most people, having an audio input jack is a much simpler solution.

Based on conversations and taking a look around the YouTube community from this year, the Canon Rebel series (T3i, T4i, and T5i) seems to be the go-to camera for YouTubers. The camera that I would recommend is the T3i as it has a flip-out monitor, audio input jack and even has the same image sensor as a 60D.

YouTube superstar iJustine posted an Instagram photo showing her vlogging cameras with the caption: "It all has to fit in my purse :); GoPro for all those quick wide-angle shots. Canon XA10 when you need a mic input and autofocus + lots of zoom! Pink Canon SD960 = best vlogging camera - perfect audio for concerts and windy settings, quick focus! With the Canon S110 - better video quality than 960, audio peaks if it's too loud and you can hear the autofocus lens in playback. The mic is on the front so if it's windy, don't even bother - it's best for b-roll and photos! The end."

If you're interested in going the iPhone route, I highly recommend the online course "iPhone Video Hero" by Jules Watkins. Ultimately, your camera is just a tool. Everybody has their favorite tools and certain tools work better for certain situations. Start with a camera you already have, or find one that you can afford (ideally with a mic input!) and get started. If you're looking for a place to start:

i. ENTRY LEVEL DSLR: Canon T5i.

Cost: Around $1,000 with kit lens. If you want to save even more money, you could buy a used T3i, which is essentially the same camera, or look for a T2i, which is basically the same camera but without a flip-out screen. The flip-out screen will always come in handy.

ii. MID-RANGE VIDEO CAMERA: Canon XA20.

Cost: Around $2000. This camera is used a lot around the YouTube Space and almost everybody shoots with it. If you want to save a little money, look for the XA10, which is an older model but essentially the same camera. Both of these cameras have a cool detachable handle that mounts on the top that gives you XLR audio inputs and manual audio controls. These cameras also have cool infrared features that you can use if you're into that kind of thing.

iii. ENTRY LEVEL PRO: Canon C100.

Cost: $5,000. In my opinion, the Canon Cinema line continues the DSLR revolution. These cameras keep a lot of the great features and image quality we got from DSLRs, but bring back the features we'd been missing from video cameras: manual audio controls, focus peaking, waveforms, long record times, and no overheating.

Microphone

Never underestimate the power of good audio. Don't have mis-steps in this department and always look for ways to improve. The on-camera mic is not going to cut it.

If your videos feature a lot of talking-head stuff in controllable locations, I highly recommend you pick up a wired lavalier mic. Do a search on Amazon and you can find decent ones as low as $20. You can also upgrade to the Sennheiser Evolution G3 wireless mic system.

Another popular choice in the YouTube community is the Rode VideoMic Pro. This is a microphone that mounts to your camera and does a pretty good job of picking up whatever sounds are directly in front of it. It's not ideal, but it is better than trying to use the on-camera mic.

There are a lot of affordable options for getting decent sound, but, unlike cameras, this is an area where spending more money really does make a huge difference in quality.

Something to Stabilize Your Camera

You're going to need something to keep your camera steady. Nobody wants to see shaky handheld footage. A tripod is your best bet. These can range from five dollars to tens of thousands of dollars. If your budget is really low, you can probably find a used photo tripod at a garage sale. You won't be able to do smooth camera movements with it, but it will hold your camera still.

The Lollipod ($50-60) is an excellent entry-level tripod that is also designed to work as a monopod or light stand. These are lightweight and fold down really small making them great for travel. Add on a Glif tripod mount or Universal Phone Holder and you will be all set for shooting great video with your phone.

As the name implies, a monopod is a one-legged camera support. Monopods are great for travel and event shooting where you need to move fast but want to avoid shaky footage.

Lights (Maybe)

If you are going to be shooting outdoors or have a "set" with lots of natural light, you might be able to get away with no additional lights. Most people are going to need a simple light set-up.

i. Basic Lighting Kit: Cowboy Studio makes some really inexpensive light kits. They come in lots of different configurations, but you can usually get a kit with 3 softbox lights from around $250. I recommend compact fluorescent Daylight Balanced photo bulbs. They stay pretty cool and will match the daylight from any nearby windows. The build quality is not great on these kits so don't expect them to last forever, but they will get you up and running and, at this price, you can easily replace the pieces that break.

ii. LED Lights: These are more expensive, but can be a lot of fun to work with. Litepanels is the king of these types of lights. These options are definitely the "bottom shelf" when it comes to lighting. Lights and related gear can get very expensive very quickly. My suggestion is to start with the bare minimum and see if you can make it work. Upgrade only when you really need to. If you have your eye on something expensive, rent it and try it out before you buy it.

Editing

Fear (or hatred) of editing is probably the second biggest obstacle to getting your YouTube channel up and running. I hear from people all the time about how much they hate editing, and I've never really understood it.

During production, just about anything can go wrong and there are often elements you have no control over, but once you're in post-production, you can focus on what you've got. It's time to take all that footage you shot and sculpt and polish it into a finished piece that your audience will love. The software has gotten so good, that it's almost as easy to edit videos, as it is to make a PowerPoint presentation. For this stage, you're going to need a computer and some editing software. Once again, there are no excuses. You can edit video on an iPhone or iPad now. Most computers come with some sort of free editing software. On Mac, it is iMovie, and on Windows, it is MovieMaker. If you don't like those, you've got more choices than ever now.

1. ScreenFlow

As its name implies, the primary purpose of ScreenFlow is screen recording. If you're doing any type of software demonstration videos, or just want to show what's happening on your computer screen, you need to get ScreenFlow. Over time, ScreenFlow has developed a surprisingly robust set of editing features. It's gotten so good that some video creators use ScreenFlow exclusively. If your show has a relatively simple format (vlogs, product demonstration, or fitness videos, etc) ScreenFlow could be the perfect tool for the job. It's got a great interface for editing audio and video tracks and comes packed with easy-to-use titles and transitions. If you're on a budget (and on a Mac) grab a copy of ScreenFlow and get to work.

2. Final Cut Pro X

FCPX is probably the most controversial editing software ever. Apple's overhaul of the much-loved Final Cut Pro was not received well by the editing community and has fallen out of grace with the majority of professional editors. That being said, it's still one of the best software.

The interface is particularly well suited to short-form content. FCPX has several core features that can take some getting used to if you've spent much time with other Non-Linear Editors. One of its key differentiating features is the magnetic timeline. Instead of a bunch of different tracks that are all of equal importance, FCPX uses the concept of a storyline. It's almost like a tube that you put the clips into in the order you want them to appear in the finished piece. FCPX automatically fills in the gaps.

You can also throw just about any type of footage into FCPX and the software will figure out what to do with it. There are very few pop-up windows asking you to supply information. Just import the footage and get to work. Apple has released free updates for FCPX every couple of months and some of them have included some pretty massive new features. If you haven't checked it out in a while, it might be time to give it another look.

3. Adobe Premiere

Adobe Premiere has picked up the gauntlet from Final Cut Pro 7 and become the NLE of choice for many professional editors. It's only available as part of the Adobe Creative Cloud, so there is a monthly subscription fee. As part of the subscription, you also get access to all of the Adobe Creative Suite, which includes essentials like Photoshop and Audition.

If your project will have lots of motion graphics generated by Adobe After Effects, Premiere should definitely be your top choice. This is a big application and it does a lot. If you've never edited before, there will be a learning curve, but once you get up and running, you won't regret having learned it.

Post-Production

There are a lot of steps involved in post-production. Here's a super-simplified post-production workflow:

- Import footage

- Edit footage

- Add transitions and text

- Customize card

- Add music

- Balance audio levels

- Color correct footage

- Add intro title sequences

Some of those steps may only take a few minutes, but they add up, especially when you are doing each step for a new video every week. As you're making your videos, think about what would happen if you had to delegate the task of post-production to somebody else. Would it be possible to make a checklist that someone else could follow and successfully produce an episode?

It sounds like the opposite of creativity, but you will actually find that having a solid system in place will directly help you produce work more quickly and feel much more satisfied creatively.

Tips and Tricks

In this section, we will look at some great tips and tricks that will help increase user engagement with your YouTube videos:

Cards and End Screens

YouTube recently did away with Annotations in favor of Cards and End Screens and, when used properly, these new tools can dramatically increase engagement and subscription rates for your channel. Let's take a look at each one and discuss how they work and some best practices for using them effectively.

Cards are CTAsthat can be added anywhere in your video in order to push viewers to watch a different video/playlist of yours, watch a different channel altogether, click a link, donate, or participate in a poll. You can add up to 5 of them to a single video.

You have to be careful with how you use Cards, though. If used improperly, they can lead to decreased watch time on your videos, since you're basically giving the user an exit! Luckily, when a user clicks a card, it opens in a new window and pauses the current video, but this could still increase your video attrition rate since the user may just end up closing the original video.

Don't be afraid to experiment and find what works best for your channel! You can monitor the performance of your Cards in YouTube's Analytics - just go to your "Creator Studio," click "Analytics" in the sidebar, and then click "Cards."

One final tip with Cards is to promote playlists over individual videos. If you are specifically trying to drive traffic to a single video, that's fine, but playlists have the added benefit of auto-playing, so theoretically your viewer is more likely to watch more than just one video!

End screens are simply calls-to-action that you can overlay during the last 20 seconds of a video in order to encourage the user to engage in some way.

Before End Screens came on the scene, creators had to manually add annotations to the end of every video. This was a tedious process and didn't look very aesthetically pleasing, plus, annotations aren't mobile-friendly so that CTAs werebasically lost if the viewer was on their phone. Considering more than half of all YouTube views come from a mobile, that's kind of a big deal.

The End Screen tool makes all of this much easier by providing a standard tool for adding calls-to-action to the end of your video. It also displays on mobile, which is a huge benefit!

In addition to a subscribed CTA and Patreon CTA, we include a link to another video in order to entice the user to keep on watching. YouTube has a handy feature where you can select a specific video to show, or you can have it determine the best video based on the viewer's prior behavior. You can also promote playlists here.

Keep it Short

During the editing process, think like a Ninja and cut anything that doesn't add to the story. As a creator, you might feel that everything you shoot is important, but you've got to be ruthless with what goes and what stays. If your first draft edit is 10 minutes long, see if you can shorten scenes or cut them entirely to get it down to 8 minutes or 5 minutes.

Provide Value to the Viewer

If your video is informative in nature, stick to the most powerful points and describe them in a brief manner. This will help the content move along quickly so the viewer doesn't get bored. If your video is more entertainment-based, make sure to keep the scenes and story moving and to keep the energy up throughout the video. As a rule of thumb, try not to stay on the same scene for more than 10 seconds.

Show Your Brand

After the intro is a great opportunity to show off your brand. Many creators opt to insert a fancy animation (once again, Fiverr is a great site for getting those on the cheap); others create their own short brand sequence just to show who they are.

Search Magnets

YouTube is the #2 search engine in the world. It might seem like if you rank well in YouTube you'd also rank well in Google, but that's not the case. When it comes to optimizing your content for search engines, we're all playing a guessing game to a certain extent. Google offers the occasional hints about what works, but the algorithm is top secret. All we can do is experiment, share the knowledge and guess some more. The YouTube search engine shares some characteristics with Google, but the current YouTube algorithm seems to be a lot simpler and much easier to crack. For this book, our focus is on ranking well on YouTube.

The following are what I believe to be the key factors that determine how videos rank in the YouTube Search Engine (until they change it).

1. Title and Metadata

They're getting closer, but as of the time of this writing, YouTube can't accurately index video content. Take a look at the default captions sometime if you don't believe me. The automated transcripts are usually pretty hilarious. Since the algorithm doesn't know what your video is about, you're going to have to tell it. The easiest way is through carefully filling out your title, description, and tags. If you neglect this step, the algorithm doesn't even know where to start. You can take this to the next level by transcribing your videos and adding text captions.

Titles and Metadata are particularly important in the first 48 hours after launching your video. At this stage, YouTube doesn't have any usage data so take advantage of this critical window. After the first 48 hours, watch time becomes the priority.

2. Watch Time

How long are viewers actually watching the videos? YouTube has officially stated that this is one of the most important factors they take into account when ranking a video. If people are bouncing off your videos within the first 30 seconds, the YouTube algorithm is going to take that as a sign that this is not a very good video (or that people are not finding what they are looking for). You can improve watch time by structuring your videos in a way that is engaging, making great thumbnails and accurately describing the video in the title, description, and tags.

Likewise, if a significant amount of viewers are spending a lot of time watching the video, this sends a signal that this is good quality content. YouTube also pays attention to Session Time. This is the overall time a user is spending on YouTube during a session. If your video leads viewers to another video (even if it's not on your channel) your channel will get partial credit. YouTube wants people to stick around on the site and watch lots of videos (and ads). If your videos promote longer overall session times, this will help boost their rankings.

3. Subscribers

Subscriber count is still important because the more subscribers you have, the faster you can get views and comments, so it ties into everything else. The first 48 hours are incredibly important and the more active and engaged subscribers you have, the easier it is to rack up a bunch of views quickly every time a video launches.

4. Comments

Comments show that the video is "alive" and that people are not only watching it, but also interacting with it. It always surprises me when people turn off comments. They are shooting themselves in the foot when it comes to generating traffic. YouTube comments can be incredibly annoying, but take them with a grain of salt and be pro-active at responding. Now that YouTube comments are integrated with Google+, they are even more important because they have a real ripple effect across Google+ and Google search.

One of the positive things to come out of the Google+ integration is the ability to blacklist certain words in your comment settings. If abusive comments are bringing you down, use the blacklist setting to filter out recurring offensive words. You can also ban trolls as they pop up. The system is far from perfect, but it's much better than it used to be, and dealing with a few negative comments is worth it for the positive effect comments can bring to your channel.

5. Back Links

Back Links are links that point to your video. They are one of the most important factors in SEO. The search engines see these links as "votes." These votes tell the robots that the content being linked to is legitimate and is what it says it is.

This was a fairly easy system to scam prior to 2009. If you had a video or blog post about "How To Fly a Kite," all you needed was a properly optimized post and more links than anybody else to be ranked #1. You could buy backlink packages on Fiverr and rank really well for pretty much anything. Google has gotten a lot more sophisticated at detecting these kinds of schemes and YouTube is getting there as well.

You can still build a legitimate web-of-links to your videos without doing anything shady. Look for areas on your platform to build relevant links. Links from other videos (in descriptions and annotations) and curated playlists are great places. You don't want your video to exist in isolation. You may notice a few recurring themes here: indicators of quality and social signals. If you're making great videos, most of these will come naturally.

6. Keywords

Before we can move forward, it's important that we nail down the concept of keywords. I've found that this concept confuses quite a few people at first. I don't think "keyword" is a very accurate description, but it is industry terminology at this point so we're stuck with it.

A keyword is a word (or phrase) that people type into a search engine when they're looking for information. Certain words (or phrases) get typed in a lot of times so those become highly coveted keywords. High traffic keywords can bring in a TON of traffic if you rank well for them.

My advice is to think about keywords in pre-production. Don't let it affect the content you're going to produce, but use it as another tool to build an audience for your project. When people use a search engine, they have a "problem," and they are looking for a "solution." Example: Someone doesn't know how to poach an egg and they need to figure out how to do it. They type in "How to poach an egg," and the search engine tries to provide them with the best solution to their problem. If your video is the first result, you're going to get a lot of views to your video. The topic of keywords may seem to apply only to how-to or instructional types of videos, but it can be a powerful tool for all kinds of projects.

7. Keyword Research

Once you start thinking about Search Engine Optimization, it's easy to get distracted by all kinds of tools and online classes promising awesome results in return for varying amounts of money. My advice is to keep it simple and not get sidetracked. Keyword research should only add a few minutes to your production time for each video. Keep in mind that you're a video creator first, and the SEO skills you are developing are there to help get your work to a bigger audience.

With that in mind, here's a quick and simple technique for Keyword Research. As an example, we're going to use a video about how to poach eggs.

Launch the Google AdWords Keyword Planner - It's free, but you have to sign up for an AdWords account.

Click "Search for New Keywords and Group Ideas." - Type a few words and phrases into "Your Product or Service" box. Keep it quick and don't over-think it or over-do it. I typed in "How to poach an egg" "Poached eggs" and "How to poach eggs." Under "Customize Your Search >> Keyword Options" check the box for "Only Show Options Closely Related to My Search." This will help keep the search narrowed down. Click "Get Ideas."

Evaluate the Keywords - The tool will give you a list of potential keywords, along with data about monthly searches. You'll also notice a column for Competition. (The Competition ranking is not about how hard it will be to outrank the other terms; instead, it refers to how competitive the term is when it comes to buying paid AdWords ads, so don't let a high competition scare you off. That just means the ads running on your video will bring in more money.) I'm mainly interested in Global Monthly Searches so I prioritize by that.

Decide What Keyword to Target - In this case, it looks like there are quite a few searches for "How to poach an egg" so that's what I'm going to target but, take a look at some of the other keywords that Google is suggesting. If you're just starting out (and your channel is not yet very authoritative), I would suggest targeting keywords that have low competition and at least 3,000 - 5,000 global monthly searches.

By just taking a few minutes to check the Google

Keyword tool, we've discovered that "How to poach an egg," has the potential to bring in a lot more traffic than "How to poach eggs" or "Poached eggs." They're all an accurate description of the video, so let's target the one that potentially will bring in more viewers.

If you have a keyword or phrase in mind before you shoot your video, work the keyword into the dialog of the video in a natural way. This will give you an extra edge if you have your videos transcribed and captioned.

Keys for Running a YouTube Channel

Your channel is what sells your videos to people. Your channel needs to entice people in so that they're interested enough to watch your videos. In this section, we will look at the most important tips for running a YouTube Channel. The first step, of course, is to make sure that every aspect of your channel is refined and every little thing is taken care of. So, here's how you can sell your brand with your channel:

Create an Eye-catching YouTube Banner:

One thing that most successful YouTubers have in common is that they all have interesting and well thought out channel banners. After all, it's the first thing viewer's see when they land on your channel page.

Now, you might be thinking "but I'm not a designer" or "I don't have money for professional photos"; well, believe it or not, it's actually possible to create an eye-catching, well-designed channel banner for next to nothing, and you don't have to be a professional designer to do it!

First off, let's talk about what makes a good channel banner. The best channel banners are very simple. They typically rely on a solid background color or a subtle gradient, which helps ensure that the imagery and message stand out.

A good banner also explains the purpose of your channel. Whether your channel is about business, travel, gaming, home decor or anything else, the goal of your channel should be clearly stated in your banner in as few words as possible. Lastly, a good banner fits your brand. It should follow a similar color scheme to other assets of your brand like your avatar, website, business cards, and so on.

One thing to keep in mind when designing your channel banner is that YouTube shows your banner at different sizes depending on what device the viewer is on, whether it's the desktop, mobile or tablet app.

There are also plenty of free graphics programs out there that you can use to design your awesome banner. Canva is a great browser-based app that makes it easy to design YouTube banners, as well as social media posts, business cards, presentations and more. There's also GIMP and Vectr, which are a bit more complicated to use, but are also completely free.

Channel Trailer

Another area where new YouTubers fail to maximize their channel is with their channel trailer. Your channel trailer works just like the trailer for a movie. It explains what your channel is all about and what the viewer can expect to see if they subscribe. It's one of the most important aspects of your YouTube channel for converting viewers to subscribers. Here's a guide you can use for creating a solid channel trailer:

1. Start with a warm introduction: Introduce yourself to your future viewers, tell them who you are and where you're from. Don't be afraid to show off your personality!

2. Explain what viewers can expect to see if they subscribe to your channel and how often you upload new videos. Upload schedules are extremely important and keep viewers coming back.

3. Don't forget to ask the viewer to subscribe! After all, that's the whole point of the trailer, right? Keep your trailer short and sweet.

4. Some trailers are 20-30 seconds long, others are

1-2 minutes, but they are rarely longer than that.

5. Remember, this may be the viewer's first encounter with your channel, so your trailer should be short, informative and full of personality!

Create Playlists

Playlists are basically collections of videos that you put together under a single category. Once you've got a few playlists, you can organize them on your channel page for viewers to browse through, almost like flipping through TV shows.

Another really important aspect of playlists is that when one video ends, the next one auto plays. This means that, when a viewer starts watching a playlist, they are more likely to keep on watching after a video ends, rather than just closing the page.

Having playlists on your channel also helps you seem more established because it feels like you have a lot of content to choose from, but make sure you give it a descriptive title, as well as a description that's chock full of keywords you'd like to target. This will help potential viewers find it! We'll talk more about Search Engine Optimization and how easy, but powerful, it is a little later.

Fill Out the About Section and Channel Keywords

Your channel's About Section gives you another opportunity to explain what your channel is all about. I recommend keeping this to only 2-3 powerful sentences, and don't be afraid to add a dash of personality! You can also use this section to explain your upload schedule and ask viewers to subscribe to your channel.

You can add keywords to your channel as well, which can help users to discover your YouTube channel when they make searches on Google, YouTube, and other search engines.

Channel Watermark

Your branding watermark is a small image that sits at the bottom right of your videos. When new viewers hover over this watermark, they see a big subscribe button. Many YouTubers put their logo or avatar down here, but we've opted to put a "subscribe" graphic on ours so that it's a little more obvious what this watermark is for.

Chapter Seven

Tools for YouTube

Here's a little secret weapon that all the YouTube pros are using: Tools. Once you start using these tools, you will get a huge leg up on the competition because it will enable you to see things like revenue projections of other channels, subscriber growth, future growth predictions, and a ton of other things. These apps can also help you when posting your videos by providing insight into keywords, title, and cross-promotion you can use to maximize views and search engine optimization. Some even help you make real money!

Before you do anything else, take a look at these tools and what they offer. They are all (mostly) free and can really take your YouTube game to the next level.

VidIQ

VidIQ can be installed as an add-on for Chrome or Firefox browsers and gives you immediate access to detailed stats on any video or channel page.

Having the VidIQ extensions is like having

superpowers. It allows you to analyze any video (including your own) to see how much money it makes, how much it's been shared on other social networks, how well it's optimized for search and a ton of other stuff. There is one drawback, however: it is a bit of a behemoth and will cause your pages to load a bit slower.

In addition, VidIQ adds a ton of useful information to your YouTube search results page. You can use it to help you find new keywords to target and to see whom you're competing with.

VidIQ also adds useful tools to your video upload page like recommended tags and similar videos. This is really useful because it often suggests tags you hadn't thought of yet, and the similar videos section offers a great opportunity for cross-promoting. The thinking is that if you include the same tags and keywords, then you are more likely to appear in the suggested videos sidebar next to that similar video.

The free version only provides basic tag and video suggestions, but if you want to unlock all the power of VidIQ, consider upgrading to a paid plan, so, basically, if you're using YouTube without this add-on, you're doing it wrong.

TubeBuddy

TubeBuddy is similar to VidIQ and offers quite a few of the same features, so I won't hash them all out again. I recommend trying both and deciding for yourself which one is the most helpful and loads the quickest.

SocialBlade

SocialBlade isn't an add-on, but it's an absolutely essential tool to include in your YouTube arsenal. This site ranks all YouTube channels and provides detailed insights into their growth and future growth potential. It even guesses at their potential monthly revenue, although it's very much a generalized figure.

You can use SocialBlade to get a handy comparison on how your channel stacks up to others in your niche. This will help you get an idea of how you're growing in comparison to other successful channels, or channels that are around your size.

You can also use SocialBlade's future projections to get a sense of how well you can expect your channel to grow in the future. Just keep in mind that these are generalized figures and will change drastically based on the growth of your channel, but they at least give you a ballpark idea.

If this seems like a lot to process, here are some things you can use SocialBlade for:

- Comparing your channel to others in order to decide if a collaboration would be beneficial for both parties.

- To see how your channel will grow in the future, in order to better pitch yourself to brand partnerships.

- To compare your growth to the growth of larger channels in your similar niche. This will give you an idea of if you are on a similar track or not.

Gleam

Running contests and giveaways on your channel can be a great way to increase views and subscribers, and Gleam is an excellent tool for doing just that. It provides an interface for users to enter your contest or giveaway with one single click, and gives you comprehensive tools for tracking entries, sharing your contest and picking winners.

Famebit

Famebit is a service that connects creators to brands who are seeking a partnership. These partnerships can be in exchange for the product itself or for a fee. Currently, you have to have at least 5,000 subscribers in order to join Famebit as a creator.

YouTube Creator Studio

YouTube offers a handy little app for your phone called the YouTube Creator Studio, which gives you access to all of your channel analytics and details on the go! This app is an absolute must-have for any YouTube creator. It makes responding to and managing comments much easier, allows you to manage your videos and playlists, and gives you access to analytics insights that are harder to find on the web version of YouTube. Best of all, it's free!

Chapter Eight

YouTube Analytics and Collaboration

In this section, we'll be looking at two important tools for increasing your engagement and revenue – Analytics and Collaborations with other YouTubers.

Analytics

This part of YouTube typically sends new creators running for the hills, and for good reason. The Analytics tab in your creator dashboard can be a daunting button to press, since when you do you're faced with charts, graphs and tons of sub-sections, but allow me to put your mind at ease. Analytics are actually really easy to understand, as long as you know what to look for.

When you start a fresh channel and load up your analytics dashboard, there isn't going to be much there so, before you can start drawing conclusions from your analytics data, you've got to get some views on your channel. In the previous chapter, we discussed how to drive initial traffic to your channel, so if you haven't already put those steps into place, do those now!

Once you've been able to get at least a few hundred views, you can start checking into your analytics to see what you can find! One important thing to keep in mind is that YouTube Analytics data is delayed. This means that you won't see channel data as it happens, but about 2 days later. Just keep in mind that anything you're seeing in your analytics dashboard is missing the last two days of data.

There is, however, a Real-time section in the YouTube Analytics Dashboard, which will give you stats on the last 24 hours of views. This data is more limited than historical data, but it can, at least, give you an idea of how a video is performing right this moment and where your views are coming from.

Watch Time

In recent years, YouTube has been tweaking its algorithm to focus more on watch time. Watch time can be defined as the number of minutes that a viewer spends while seeing a video so, if you have a channel with 10-minute videos, but generally users only watch half of this, which is 5 minutes of your video, then the average watch time can be said to be 5 minutes, or basically 50%.

For YouTube, a channel with a higher watch time means more revenue because the channel can clearly hold a viewer's attention. Most importantly, it's actually about the number of minutes that are being watched rather than the percentage of a video. As an example, say there's a channel that has a 75% watch time on average, and if the videos on the channel are short and only 2 minutes long, then viewers might be watching most of the video, but it's still not a lot of minutes.

Some YouTubers came up with a clever solution to this problem; they started making videos that were far longer than normal. This has definitely reduced the quality of videos on YouTube since the overall quality is reduced. Most people just add content to their videos for no reason but to stretch the video. At the end of the day though, it's helping YouTube make more money, and hence helping you make money too.

Watch time percentage is not completely useless either, as compared to say the total watch time. You should always aim to increase your percentage watch time because, at the end of the day, it means that viewers are seeing more of your videos. This is why you should continuously monitor this metric and the changes that happen with respect to it.

I believe that 50% watch time, in general, is a good mark to shoot for on any given video so, if your videos are 6 minutes long, you should aim for a watch time of 3 minutes.

One way to improve your watch time is to experiment with tweaking your video format and content quality. The goal is to make your videos more useful, which is one of the best things you can do to improve watch time! You can also try to incorporate cliffhangers. We'll often mention something really fun we're going to do later on in the video, with the hopes that it will entice viewers to stick around to see it.

Other Metrics to Watch

Watch time may be the most important metric, but it's not the only one you should be watching. Here's a list of the most important metrics to track in your Analytics Dashboard:

Watch time/video length - As we've already discussed, the more a viewer is watching, the more effective a video is, and YouTube rewards that.

Subscriber to view ratio - This is an indication of how engaging your videos are to your subscriber base. If you have 1,000 subscribers, and a video gets 100 views, that's a 10% subscriber-to-view ratio. In my opinion, you should shoot for a minimum of 10%, but you can also try to shoot for 20-30%.

Video views in the first 24 to 48 hours - This also indicates how engaged your subscribers are, and how quickly your video begins ranking in search. One great way to increase this is to push your subscribers to enable notifications! This ensures they get a push notification on their phone as soon as you upload a new video. Often mention this in your videos and even demonstrate exactly how to do it.

Traffic sources - How are people finding your video? If you know, then you can try to exploit that source and increase traffic even more.

Some traffic sources are a bit cryptic. What the heck are "Browse features" and "YouTube channels" anyway? There's a handy guide from YouTube that explains what each one is and you can find it online.

Traffic locations - Your content might be resonating more with a specific country. Make sure you monitor geographic traffic sources in analytics too. If your content is resonating with people in Central America, for example, it might be worth it to translate your videos into Spanish or make specific videos for that audience.

Your most popular videos - Always look for which videos have the highest total views and daily views and try to figure out why these videos are doing so well.

You can find these front and center under the "Overview" section of your Analytics Dashboard. Once you've identified your most successful videos, start digging into their individual analytics and look at their traffic sources, watch time, like/comment rate and more in order to see if you can uncover any patterns that you can replicate.

Collaborating with Other YouTube Channels

This is an area that can lead to huge growth for your channel, but it's also sometimes difficult to pull off. A collaboration is simply when two YouTubers come together to make a video. They typically create separate videos for each channel and promote each other's videos on their social media outlets once posted. Collaborating with other YouTubers does a few specific things that can lead to some big-time growth.

It exposes you to a new audience. If a YouTuber has an engaged subscriber base, collaborating with them means you are exposed to their viewers who have a high likelihood of subscribing to your channel. Even if the channel is smaller than you are, if their subscribers have high engagement, a collaboration could be worth it.

It builds your network. Collaborating with other YouTubers is a great way to make contacts and, more importantly, friends! This would mean that you could consistently expose your channel to their audience and vice-versa.

It gets you used to working with others. Thinking about

doing your first collaboration can be scary. What if it doesn't get any views? What if your video is just awkward? Of course, there's always that possibility, but you never know until you try. Plus, collaboration gets easier after the first time.

"Great, so collaborations sound like an awesome way to grow my channel, but how do you find people to collaborate within the first place?" This is a question you will probably ask yourself.

How to Find Collaborations

Finding collaboration partners when you first start your channel can certainly be tough. The key is creating organic relationships with other YouTubers in your genre.

Networking

First and foremost, YouTube is a social platform, which means you always have to be networking in order to create and sustain relationships. This means commenting on other YouTubers channels and videos, giving people shout-outs in your own videos, retweeting other YouTubers on YouTube, and following other YouTubers on Instagram, etc. Networking on YouTube is something that must be done daily if you want to see real results.

Reaching Out

Sometimes, it's just a matter of reaching out. If you find another YouTuber who lives in your city or state, or if you are traveling near their location, try emailing them or leaving them a comment and explain your idea for a collaboration. Even if you're not located near any other YouTubers, you could try a remote collaboration. For example, you could try splicing in some of their footage into your video, doing a tandem challenge video, a Q & A, or any other idea that relates to both of your channels.

Finding a YouTuber's email address is pretty easy. It's usually listed in their About Section under Contact Information.

Focus on Similar Size Channels

Of course, it would be great to have 1,000 subscribers and collaborate with someone with 10,000, but it's not very realistic. There's just not much in it for the other channel. The perfect collaboration is when there's something in it for both parties, so shoot for collaborating with channels close to your own subscribers/view rate.

As you grow, the gap between subscribers becomes less consequential. For example, once you're at 10,000 subscribers, you might be able to collaborate with someone who has 20,000 subscribers, and, once you're at 100,000, you might be able to collaborate with someone with 1,000,000 subscribers!

Use Channel Pages

Channel Pages is a site where you can post your own channel and other YouTubers can connect with you in order to organize potential collaborations. Brands and agencies can also browse profiles there in order to find partnerships, so you might even make some money on there!

Social Media Marketing Importance

It is no secret that videos have become a very important part of a company's marketing strategy. People log in to YouTube to search for their brand's presence and go through the videos they have uploaded. YouTube now has 3 billion+ viewers for its videos therefore making it a great place for brands to reach out to its customers. It has a global reach and about 70% of the audience is based outside of the United States. Therefore, it is quite easy to reach out to new customers. Here are a few things that make YouTube a great platform for social media marketing.

Viral Posts

YouTube is the best place to make your videos go viral. As mentioned, there are over 3 billion views per day therefore making it easier to find a large audience for your video. Be it an ad for your product or a demo, chances are high your video will go viral if you have a large subscriber base. You also have the option of redirecting people from your other social media platforms to your YouTube channel and further increasing chances of expanding your traffic and customer base.

Channels

It is possible to have your company's own channel on YouTube where you can post videos of your products and services. Make sure you create a series of videos before allowing customers to access it. Have a library of videos ready that can be played in one go so that customers feel motivated to subscribe to your channel. You have the option of editing previous videos at any time. Leave the comments section open so that you know what the audience thinks about the videos and if they have any suggestions to make it better.

Analytics

One great feature of YouTube is that it helps the channel's creator know how many views each video has received. This makes it easier to plan future videos. There will be no complications involved in tracking how the videos are doing. The number of views can be accessed by looking at the number present just below the video. This will help to instantly know how popular the video is. It will also be easy to gauge how many are viewing the video on a regular basis.

Other Uses

Additionally, YouTube also gives the option for businesses to keep an eye on the competition and know what they have been up to. It also gives them an insight into the words that should be used to popularize their videos and make it more accessible to customers.

Using YouTube Live

Promoting Productsand Services

Now that we looked at the benefits of using YouTube as a social media tool, here is looking at what YouTube live can do for you.

YouTube live, like Facebook live, allows you to host live videos on your channel. You can broadcast it live to your audience. The content can be anything of your choice as long as it is addressing their expectations. It can be a demonstration video of the products; it can be a video showcasing the various features of the product etc. Hosting a live video will always prove to be a great way to engage your audience and get more customers on board.

Additionally, these videos can be quite informative and push your sales upwards. There might be some viewers who have never heard about your product before watching the videos. This will push them to buy the product if they like the video you have put up.

YouTube live can also be used to tease a product or build hype around it such that it pushes up the audience's curiosity. It can be used to demonstrate a new product that is yet to be launched in the market.

The platform can also be used to host contests and give away so that it keeps the audience hooked. This can also aid in brand awareness and make it easier for the audience to find you.

Live Streamduring Events

A great time for you to go live is during events. By going live during events, you have the chance to show your audience what is happening at the event and behind the scenes activities. Whenever you are having a show or an event then it will be vital to host a live video for your audience. Live events always raise up people's curiosity and they will tune in to see what is being streamed. If you hold events and sell tickets for the same, then it will be even more important to stream. It is estimated that about 67% of the people who watch live streams of events are likely to buy tickets to the show. That is a majority of your audience and thus, it is extremely important to host live videos for your shows.

This is especially imperative for companies that are a part of the entertainment industry so that it is easy to drive up sales. But live shows should be a part of all businesses marketing strategies.

The event can be small or big depending on the product that is being sold.

Offering Exclusive Content

Use YouTube live to offer your customers content that is exclusive and can only be sought through the live video. This will give your audience a sense of exclusivity and make them come back for more. They will feel like they were a part of a video that was exclusive for them. This will make them feel special. But you must give them information that they will not get anywhere else and you should make it obvious to them. Try to be creative and provide information of value. Let the audience tell you what they would like to see so that you can incorporate their suggestions in the video. It can be a video on the everyday functioning of the firm, which will give them a glimpse into what goes on behind the scenes. This will bring them closer to the company and understand what actually goes on.

Keeping the Audience Engaged

Do your best to keep the audiences engaged with the content you provide. It should not be too boring as otherwise they might not come back for it. Make sure the content is enthralling and has all the requisite elements that make videos engaging for the audience. A good idea is to go through videos of popular YouTubers and seeing how they present their content. Channel some of their elements so that it is easier to please your audience.

Pre-plan the video and don't go about it on an impulse. Not only will you end up streaming to a lesser audience but also give them content that is mediocre. It might change their perception and you might end up losing subscribers thinking you are spamming them.

Make use of all the features that YouTube live offers you to make the most of it. There are many built-in features that can be beneficial to you. There are poll options that can be used to know what your audience is looking for. It can also be used at the end of the video to know how many liked the video.

Live videos can help companies create a more genuine interaction with customers as compared to traditional ways of answering to their comments. This can make it easier for you to not only plant yourself in the customer pool in a better way but also know exactly what they are looking for.

New Features

New features have been introduced that makes it easier for people to broadcast live videos on YouTube. It is easier for people to now broadcast live using their phones. This is especially useful if other platforms like Facebook is down and you have to broadcast a live video. You can use YouTube live from just about anywhere and keep your promise of broadcasting a live video.

As you can see, YouTube live can be used to grow your business and attract a larger audience base.

Chapter Nine

YouTube Advertising

You can make money just by making and uploading YouTube videos. YouTube runs ads on your videos and they pay you a percentage of what they make. This is usually the first income stream that new YouTubers pursue. It's definitely the easiest and possibly the fastest.

We've all heard stories of people getting rich from their YouTube channels, but it's difficult to find out what people are actually making on YouTube. Those numbers we see online might be exciting if you're just starting out and have a low overhead but, when you factor in the incredible amount of time and work that goes into creating a show and building an audience, these numbers are really low. This is why I never recommend starting a YouTube channel primarily as a way to make money.

The YouTube ad system is driven by the concept of CPM. CPM stands for cost per mille or Cost Per Thousand views. Individual views aren't worth much, but advertisers are willing to pay for them in batches of a thousand. It's really what makes the whole YouTube ecosystem work. If you have a mega-channel, you can do pretty well with this but, unless your videos are generating hundreds of thousands of views on a regular basis, it's going to be difficult to scale this income stream up to something you can make a decent living on.

If you're familiar with Google's AdSense system, you'll have an idea of how the YouTube Ad system works. The majority of it actually is Adsense. Advertisers set up campaigns targeting certain keywords, interests and demographics and place bids (auction-style) for ad placements. Some keywords are very competitive and can cost quite a bit.

Why CPM is Great for Advertisers and Lousy for Creators

Let's break down how CPM works a little more. Say there's a hypothetical "How To Fly A Kite" video that has been up on YouTube for over a month, and it got, say, 10,000 views. If your channel is new but has an average search term, if you're lucky you might get a $5 CPM.

So 10,000 views/1,000 = 10 x $5 = $50.

Pretty sweet, right? Well, hold on a second. It never quite works out that way. There are a few factors to take into account before you can make any type of projection: Not all views are monetized.

Non-monetized views don't count. You can find out what views actually count by going into your YouTube Analytics and clicking on Ad Performance. The Estimated Monetized Playbacks is the number that counts.

YouTube defines it as: "*When a viewer views your video (i.e., a View) and is shown at least one ad impression or when the viewer quits watching during the pre-roll ad without ever reaching your video.*"

"$10,000 - 5,000 = 5,000$ views$/1,000 = 5$ x $\$5 = \$25$

Of course, YouTube is going to take a cut, their payment for hosting the video and maintaining the system that makes this whole thing possible; officially, that cut is 45%.

$10,000 - 5,000 = 5,000$ views$/1,000 = 5$ x $\$5 = \$25$ - $\$11.25 = \$13.75$.

These numbers are purely speculative, but it should give you an idea of how it works. After you take out the non-monetized Playbacks and then take out YouTube's percentage, the CPM that actually goes into your pocket is pretty low.

The part that can be discouraging is that (unless you have a viral smash) it takes a long time and a lot of work to make a significant amount of income. This is a long-term play.

Once you start to hit a good number of views, everything looks a little bit different. You have money to reinvest into the business and there's a sense of validation that comes with it, so, even though building a decent revenue stream through YouTube takes a lot of work and time, there are benefits above and beyond just the income. Use your YouTube earning numbers as a way to set goals, push yourself further and make your channel better.

Chapter Ten

LinkedIn

LinkedIn is a very powerful platform in this age for anyone who wants to boost their professional status and make connections with like-minded, ambitious individuals. It gives you lots of advantages as a professional, so it becomes paramount to be aware of the potential of this platform and know how to use it to your advantage.

Everyone uses LinkedIn these days, from individuals to businesses to non-profit organizations. Everyone understands the power of a brand and so they all want to reap its benefits by making a name for themselves. LinkedIn is an amazing tool to help in this area.

Quick Tips

In this section, we will take a look at some simple, easy to follow tips that you can act upon quickly. It will take you very little time, say, around 8-10 minutes each, so you can even do these when you take breaks from work.

Use a Recent, Professional Photo

Your photo is a window into your personality as it can tell the other person a lot about you. In our world, appearances play a huge role, so you'd be wise not to underestimate the role a good, professionally-clicked photograph plays in attracting people to your profile. Countless studies have been conducted in this regard, and the general conclusion seems to be that professional-looking photos of your torso are the best.

To get around to this, discard that cropped party-time photo (or worse, a selfie) that you have as your profile photo at the moment, and put up a professionally clicked photo. It will inspire confidence and trust in people who see your profile.

Use a Good Headline

When people visit your profile, one of the first things that they notice is your headline, so it goes without saying that the headline is one of the most important parts of your profile. Now, if you've been using LinkedIn for a few years, you might have noticed that every time you change your job, LinkedIn defaults to the job title as your profile headline. This, admittedly, is not the greatest way to appeal to recruiters. You need something personal, unique, and compelling, so you should think about a new, powerful headline for your profile each time you change your job or get promoted.

This keeps your profile fresh and appealing.

Follow the Right People

To stay in the know and always ahead of average Joes, you need to be aware of what the top personalities in your industry are up to. The industry leaders are the people who influence the world and bring change, and this goes beyond, as they inspire success in others, so make sure you're following the right people on LinkedIn. This helps you get valuable advice and relevant news on a daily basis. Regardless of your industry or experience level, you have to start somewhere, so don't worry too much about it. Just start with a few key personalities and then build it up from there.

Keep Your Current Responsibilities Updated

This one is exceptionally important for those who have recently changed jobs or have been promoted. When that happens, the person is so busy getting used to their current role and responsibilities that social networking can take the back seat. With a new job comes the need to update your profile so it reflects your current responsibilities and job profile. Nobody wants to contact a person on LinkedIn to fill in for a particular role only to later find out that the person contacted is not actually handling the necessary responsibilities at their current job.

Always keep your current position, job title, location, and responsibilities all up-to-date. Whenever possible, add some media content to your profile to demonstrate and show your work off to potential recruiters. This works as a portfolio and also makes your profile look aesthetically more pleasing. Double score!

Curate Your Groups

LinkedIn suggests some groups that may be relevant to you and your industry when you first register as a user. Most people skip this part at the get-go, and a few decide to join every single one suggested by the site. That's okay. A new user doesn't know any better, but most of us don't go back to a group after joining it.

I want to tell you that groups are actually really important to be a part of the community and make more meaningful connections, so log in to your LinkedIn account at least once a day and go through some posts in your favorite groups. Also, take a few moments to go over all your groups so you know which ones are irrelevant or useless now and you can delete them. You don't have to check *all* your groups because that can be excessively time-consuming. Just pick 2-3 groups that you find interesting and check those.

Also, join your university's alumni group if there exists

any. Staying connected to your roots is very beneficial, as you always know what's going on at your university and what kind of people are coming out. You can network with freshers and find new talent for your own ventures, and you can even find some career advancement opportunities in these groups, so stay on the lookout!

Ask for a Recommendation

When you go for interviews, after clearing a couple of rounds, you make it to a stage where your prospective employers are bound to ask you for some references. In those situations, LinkedIn recommendations work like a charm. They're perfect because they are by people who already think highly of you and have endorsed you for the skills you've taken the interviews for. They are social proof of things you are good at.

This is why LinkedIn recommendations are so important. They increase your reputation when they come from reputed people with a good work ethic, so make sure you reach out to some people on LinkedIn you've worked closely within the past or currently work with. They can be your co-workers, supervisors, or even clients. Make sure your request is personal and polite. You can mention why the particular person is perfect for writing a recommendation for you. This will make them feel special and increase your chances of getting a good recommendation, and don't forget to write them a recommendation in return.

Filter Your Endorsements

People on LinkedIn endorse each other for skills quite often, so the chances are you'll also get endorsed for a lot of skills regularly if you have a decent sized network. As a beginner, we often add everything we're endorsed for in our profile, and this leads to skewed metrics when people visit our profile and see our endorsed skills. This is why you need to filter out some endorsements that shouldn't be there, at least not on the top. Some skills look great at the top because they are relevant to your industry. Others, like Microsoft PowerPoint and the likes, don't look so great, so take time to filter such endorsements out.

Connect With Your Team

This is hands down the easiest thing to follow in all the tips mentioned in this chapter. All you need to do is look up your colleagues on LinkedIn and then connect with them. If your team is fairly large, like a whole department, that's great. If it is very small, you could look at connecting with people beyond your team too. Just make sure you know these people on *some* level. If you do connect with people you don't know well, you could use this as an opportunity too. You just need to embrace it and not be awkward about it. This is a chance for you to say hello and get to know the person by asking them out for a tea or coffee.

Chapter Eleven

LinkedIn Profile

Here's the thing about any social media profile you use professionally – if you're not visible to people you're targeting, it doesn't matter how great your profile looks. People should be easily able to find you. Moreover, people should see *you* when they search for people of your trade, be it on LinkedIn or on a regular search engine. For that, you have to make it a priority to tweak your profile in such a way that it becomes more visible.

In LinkedIn, you have a profile that can be seen by anyone, regardless of whether they are a LinkedIn user or not. This is because your profile has two components. One is visible only to LinkedIn users and the other is visible to everyone who looks for you on the Internet.

Now, to improve the visibility of your profile, you need to look at both the components of your profile. Our goal is to have such an excellent public profile that people just can't resist checking your full profile. Keeping that in mind, let's take a look at some tips you can use to increase your profile's visibility.

Revise Your Public Profile Settings

We want to make sure your profile shows up when people search for you on the Internet. To do that, we have to check the profile settings in LinkedIn. Go to Privacy & Settings on your homepage. From there, you can manage your profile settings. Click on the 'Edit Your Public Profile' button and see what items are shown there. You can choose which items you want visible to people using a public search. On the right side, you can see the items visible on your private profile.

Now, what things you decide to show to the public are completely up to you. Some people prefer going fully transparent and making all sections of their private profile visible publicly. That is okay. On the other hand, others choose to show only a few sections publicly so as to give the viewer a brief overview. That's okay too. Whatever you choose to do depends on the type of work you do and the degree of public visibility you're fine with.

One thing you need to remember is that rich-text media will never be visible in public searches, so full-text recommendations and videos are out of the picture. This is why your job experience and description are the most important parts of your profile. They attract the public viewer to check your full profile. Make sure this information is always excellent.

Use Relevant Information

Next thing you need to do is see what your profile looks like to a stranger on the web. Log out of LinkedIn and search yourself on Google. Hopefully, if you have a name that's not too common, you'll see your own LinkedIn profile as one of the first few links on the Google search results. When you click on it, you'll see the version of your profile that is visible to everyone publicly. Once you see it, you can assess what looks okay and what needs changes. There will definitely be some areas you can improve upon.

Here are some questions you need to ask yourself when looking at your public profile objectively:

- Is there any critical information missing from my public profile?

- Is there something I want my public profile to communicate that it isn't doing right now?

- Is there an important message I am not giving to the public about my work?

- Could I benefit from showing something else on my public profile?

Once you've asked yourself these questions, it's time to figure out the answers to them and write them down so you can use them later while editing your public profile again. You will also have a rough structure and database of things you can add to your profile.

The next step is obviously opening your LinkedIn account and updating your profile, so go on and check your job description, skills listed, and everything else that is important and publicly visible. You will have no difficulty tackling this since you already made a list of improvements you need to make.

Use Keywords

One of the biggest things in search engine optimization is the keyword. If you want any sort of content to be properly visible on the Internet, you need to have enough relevant keywords in it. This applies to your LinkedIn profile too. For it to be visible in public searches, it must contain certain important keywords.

The first thing you need to do is use LinkedIn's search feature to look up relevant keywords for your niche and create a list. As an example, using keywords like "sales" and "selling" is a good idea for you if sales are something your expertise includes.

The next step is to use these relevant keywords one by one and see how you rank in the search results. The further down you are in the results, the more improvements your profile needs, so look at the profiles of people who're high up on the list and take a note of the key areas. Analyze how they've used important keywords to strengthen their profile and learn from it.

The final step is to go to your own profile and edit it. Your goal is to add the important keywords to your profile without sounding redundant and as strategically as possible. You can use these keywords in your headings, summary, and job description. This will improve the visibility of your profile across the platform.

Use a Custom Profile URL

The last thing we touch upon in the whole process is your public profile URL. Your URL is unique to your profile and you should use it tactically to improve your profile's visibility even more. When you create a good profile URL, it gives your profile a boost in public search rankings. If your profile ranks higher, it will be more visible for obvious reasons, and you will get more hits. Another cool little thing you can do with it is hand it out to your clients and others in your network because it's easy to remember.

Differentiate and Capitalize

Now that your public profile is properly set up, you will start getting more attention from people in your industry that are looking for people of your expertise, but there's more to it than just people viewing your profile. This is just the first step. You want people who look at your profile to ultimately *connect* with you. That is what benefits you, right?

It is now time to differentiate your private and public profile. Your private profile needs to offer even better content so the viewer is pleased and impressed with your profile. This means there should be some things in your private profile, like your recommendations and other rich-text media, which is top-notch. Take the example of someone who uses YouTube as part of their job. They can definitely benefit from sharing some of the best videos in their private profile.

You can even add photos and videos telling people about your work and experience. This not only increases the aesthetic value of your profile, but also creates some trust in the visitors. Don't forget to ask your friends and colleagues to write some good recommendations for you and do the same for them. This is a fantastic way to make your mark and stand out because recommendations provide social proof of your competence, and human beings in general like social proof to help them make important decisions.

Consider Going Premium

If you have the money to spare for this and really want a boost, consider going pro. With a premium plan of LinkedIn, you get a lot of new features you didn't have before, so definitely consider this.

What Not to Do

For everything you do right to improve your profile, there is twice the number of things you can do wrong. In this chapter, I've decided to list down some pretty common things you should avoid doing if you want a stellar profile.

No Spammy Messages

There's a really important thing you need to understand before you make a pitch to a potential client, investor or someone else. People hate self-serving messages. They will detect it in the first couple of lines itself and won't bother to read more, so keep this in mind and don't send spammy messages to people on LinkedIn. Take time to write messages that are well thought out and customized for different people. They should be beneficial to them. If they're not, you won't have any luck.

Only Legitimate Recommendations

This is very important to be mindful of. You must never ask people you don't know well for recommendations, and neither should you give them recommendations. This doesn't bode well for your profile. Recommendations are a way of saying you vouch for the person, so if you cannot personally vouch for someone, don't give them or ask them for a recommendation. If their reputation is poor, it will look bad on your profile too.

No Negativity in Groups

LinkedIn groups are supposed to be helpful and supportive with lots of meaningful discussions, so don't be the person who brings negativity in the group by being overly scathing and unnecessarily critical of everything. Sure, there will always be disagreements, but they don't need to be hostile. Make sure your criticism is valid, constructive, and called for.

Don't Post Too Much

LinkedIn has a very professional environment, understandably, since it's a professional network. This is not Facebook. You don't get to post a status update every time you have something new on your mind, so limit your status updates on LinkedIn to one per day and two at maximum.

No Self-Serving Content in Groups

Like I said in the previous point, groups are supposed to be positive and helpful. If you're posting self-serving spammy content there, it helps nobody. Imagine everyone doing that in the groups you're a part of. There will be no meaningful discussion in any group ever. That is in nobody's interest so, to avoid this, always craft your content for the particular forum you're posting in, and make sure it is of value to the target audience.

Don't Promote Your Facebook Page

There's a certain LinkedIn etiquette you should be aware of when using the website. It asks you to be mindful of your conduct and behave professionally at all times. One of the most common mistakes new people make on LinkedIn is to beg for "likes" on their Facebook pages. I cannot begin to describe how *lame* this is and how much it hurts your reputation. If you do this, you will be seen as desperate and good-for-nothing, so never beg for likes. Only mention your Facebook to another user when you've built a good professional relationship with them. That means messages like "Please like my page" are out of the question.

Be Careful of this Setting

"Allow recipients to see each other's names and email addresses."

This is an option when sending messages to multiple people at once. Always make sure that this is toggled off when you're sending such messages unless it's to people you already know well, and they don't care whether the message is personalized for them or not. People you don't know very well don't like getting random messages that are meant for 10 other people. They like personalized messages that make them feel special.

"I see you viewed my profile…" is a big NO.

Yes, you heard me. It's creepy as hell and doesn't make the other person want to connect with you anymore. In fact, if anything, it only hurts your chances, so don't start your messages to people by saying this. If you want to connect with someone, write a personalized message in the connection request. Do not include this phrase!

LinkedIn is Different From Other Social Networks

People often tend to forget this or are not aware of this at all, and this hurts their reputation on LinkedIn. Like I mentioned before, being on LinkedIn means you need to follow some etiquette, kind of like Reddit. The first thing you need to remember is that this is not Twitter or Facebook. It's a completely different type of network that has specific purposes, and one should not use it outside of those purposes, so don't post status updates about what you had for lunch on LinkedIn.

Don't Ask New Connections to Endorse You

You may see random people endorsing you for particular skills and realize that you hardly know this person at all. This could make you think that asking strangers and new connections for endorsements is okay, but let me tell you, it isn't. Endorse only the people you know well, and the same goes for asking for endorsements.

Do Away with Standard Invitations

Saying "I'd like to add you to my professional network" is the quickest way to tell someone they're not worth a few seconds of your time. It's boring, it's unappealing, and it turns them down, so stop using the standard invitation text and write a personal message instead. Yes, it seems like a lot of work, but it's worth the effort. Make sure you know whether the other person is already on LinkedIn or not. If they're not, offer to help them out with it. Keep the message short and to the point. You can use the same custom messages for a few people with the same expertise, but not too many of them.

Keep Your Expectations Flexible

People are different and network differently, so do not have rigid expectations when it comes to LinkedIn networking. It can cause you unnecessary frustration and discourage you from building healthy relationships with talented people. Be mindful of the following things:

1. Don't judge people for how they network. People do what they feel is right for them and hence, they have different standards when it comes to networking. Also, remember that some people network for reasons above and beyond just networking.

2. Don't expect a quick response all the time. People have lives and they are busy. Not everyone will respond in a timely manner and, with this, you should also remember that not everyone is interested in the kind of professional relationship you want. You can try from your end, but don't expect reciprocal from the other person.

3. Don't assume things when you see someone's contact list is private. They may have good

reasons to do so, and they have every right to do so too. Keeping things private is not a professional sin.

4. If you're not sure whether someone will recognize you, don't send them a connection request pronto. Try sending them an email or an SMS first to let them know you want to connect with them professionally. Hey, some people are just bad with names!

Don't Go In Unprepared

Most people who have a decent reputation in any industry will have proper information available on their profile with regards to how you should contact them. It can be both implied and direct, and you need to be aware of this before you initiate dialog with them. You have a responsibility to contact people in their preferred mode of communication and not come off as a nuisance.

Pay attention to people's profiles, review their contact settings, respect their privacy and what they're trying to convey with their profile. Listen more and speak less, figuratively speaking here. This shows that you did your homework well and took the time to prepare. People will appreciate you for it.

Don't Disregard LinkedIn Messages

LinkedIn messages are not any less important than your Facebook messages and your emails, so don't treat them like a second-class option. Many people think that LinkedIn messages are not time-sensitive or that they're not as official as a phone call or an email. They're wrong. Make sure email notifications for your LinkedIn messages are always turned on, and make sure you check your inbox daily. Respond to your messages yourself instead of delegating it or ignoring the task altogether.

Quantity is not Quality

As with most other things in life, quantity and quality are two very different things and one may not imply the other in most cases. Doing something a lot doesn't mean it is being done well. If you really want to know how well you're doing something on LinkedIn and track your progress with actual numbers, there are certain business metrics available on the website to help you out, like leads generated, interviews scheduled, public opportunities created and qualified job candidates contacted, and much more. Be sure to check them out and track your actual progress with them.

Focus on Others' Needs, Not Yours

There's a saying in marketing that says, "People don't care about your product, they only care about finding solutions to their own problems." This is a golden rule that every marketing expert will follow when marketing a particular product or service. They will tailor it in a way that shows the target audience how the product or service solves their problem effectively.

You must remember the exact same thing when it comes to LinkedIn etiquette too. People don't care what you want or what you have to say. They will only pay attention to you if you have something of value to offer to them.

Chapter Twelve

Best Practices for a

LinkedIn Profile

Now that you've covered the basics and done everything to make your profile look good, what else can you do to make it even better? And yes, you can make it even better. There are certain things that make all the difference between a good and a great profile. In this chapter, we're going to take a look at some advanced tips for people who want to take LinkedIn to an even greater level and create a 5-star LinkedIn profile.

Support Additional Languages

Some jobs are localized and don't have to offer additional language support for them to be better than the others in the industry; however, some jobs can benefit from offering support for languages other than English. If you are someone who caters to an international clientele or industry and you talk to people from other countries often, it's a good idea to make your profile available in multiple languages.

LinkedIn has a lot of languages available and you can choose any number of them, so go ahead and create multiple versions of your profile in different languages and make sure you have also updated the profile information with appropriately translated data. It will go a long way in getting you international connections.

In fact, your Summary doesn't even have to be an exact translation. You can tweak it to cater to the demographics of different countries if you know what they value most.

Rearrange Sections

Many people are now aware that in LinkedIn, they can move different sections of their profile to make it look how they please. It helps in showing the prioritized stuff first. If you know what people in your industry look for first, you can bring the relevant sections to the top. Here are some of the sections in your profile you can rearrange:

- Projects

- Publications

- Certifications

- Summary

- Additional info

- Organizations

- Experience

- Education

- Courses

Some people work in industries where prospective employers and clients don't care about where you went to school or how many degrees you have, so those people can put the Education section to the end. It can be reversed for industries where this sort of information is important and relevant.

Check Your Profile on Different Platforms

We all know that Internet usage on mobile devices has increased manifold in the last few years because of the revolution in the telecom industry. According to the latest stats, more than 50% of users check LinkedIn via a mobile, so it's important for you to take a look at how your profile appears on mobile devices.

You will obviously notice some changes and you can correct these so your profile looks great on every platform. Similarly, if you have embedded your profile anywhere, you should also check how it looks there. If you want LinkedIn widgets, you can use these from the LinkedIn Plugins page. Make sure the widgets you are using are both functional and good-looking.

Regularly Publish Posts

Blogging on LinkedIn is still fairly new, but it's a powerful means to make a name for yourself and establish yourself as an influencer in your industry. If you churn out quality posts regularly, you will be seen as a thought leader. People will look up to you and they will await your posts with eagerness.

Make sure you think of new topics to write about each week or every two weeks, and then research them to find lots of relevant data. Write down a well-crafted post and publish it with a relevant, catchy image. This will surely get you attention from people in your industry if you publish quality posts consistently. Make sure you stay away from easy, overly done topics that nobody cares about anymore. Quality trumps quantity every time.

With these tips, you will build an absolute powerhouse of a profile, so take some time out of your daily schedule and get down to these things. The effort will pay off, I promise.

Social Media Marketing Importance

Not many businesses realize the importance of using LinkedIn as a social media-marketing tool. Here are some reasons to use it to promote your business.

Search Engine Reputation Management (SERM)

Google provides LinkedIn the privilege of showing up higher on search results so that it is easier to find it on the search page. It will be easier for customers and other collaborators to look for you, as all they have to do is type in your name and find you high on top of the results page. If you wish to protect certain aspects on the page, then it will be important to know what to publish on the page so that it is easier to manage the content and what will be displayed to the public.

Increasing Brand Visibility

By increasing your connections and adding your

employees and board members and taking active part in-group discussions about the company, it will be easier to make your brand more visible.

Generate Leads

By taking part in the LinkedIn community, you will have the golden chance to increase your leads. You will be in direct contact with people who can help to push your business forward and upwards. If you have a link to your company's white paper, then provide it to the audience so that they know exactly what your company is all about and can connect with you.

Job Switching

It will be easy for you to track people when they switch jobs. Once you connect with the audience and find the right personnel, you can know what they are up to and track their career movement. This will help you find new leads in their new company based on their new connections.

Target Ads

LinkedIn gives you the power to use text ads to pursue individuals that you consider to be good prospects to run your business. This can be HR executives and other qualified personnel capable of taking your business places. It will be easy to target them by placing the ads such that they can view them easily and reach out to people who are apt for a specific role in your business.

Finding New Talent

LinkedIn makes for a great place to find new talent for your company. All you have to do is use specific keywords based on the profile and location of your company. As per studies, LinkedIn helps to find replacements by cutting down the time taken by almost 50%.

Product Information

LinkedIn now provides the feature of placing products and services on the page by linking them to the websites and also YouTube videos. This can help customers review your products.

Chapter Thirteen

An Introduction to

Instagram

Visual communication is the new age marketing strategy with more and more brands choosing it over conventional ad display. Brands have realized the importance of using visuals to market their products in order to reach out to bigger audiences.

Many brands now make use of Instagram as their base to put out ads that are tailored to woo their customers. They leave no stone unturned in delivering ads that appeal to their current and fresh customers and try to make full use of the platform's marketing potential.

Instagram is a new platform and a baby compared to other social media platforms such as Facebook and Twitter. Yet, it is becoming massive and might end up overtaking the other platforms in terms of connectivity and popularity.

Marketing agencies now resort to using Instagram's features to create visual ads that are artistic and communicative. If you too wish to make full use of

Instagram as a portal to display company ads and increase your brand's worth, then here is a quick guide to help you understand all that you need to know about the social media platform and what it can offer to you.

Instagram is revolutionizing the way in which brands communicate with their customers. Gone are the days when brands relied on television commercials to reach out to their audiences. The new age is all for being in direct communication with customers and using visual esthetics to reach out to their target audience.

Instagram has been stepping it up ever since brands recognized its potential with more and more resorting to tactics that can put them ahead of the competition. With expectations reaching sky high, marketing agencies try to come up with interesting and innovative concepts to throw light on their products in a different way.

The platform allows agencies to tap into their creative sides and indulge in visual storytelling that can bring their audiences closer to them. Although Instagram has been around for just eight years, brands have adopted and evolved to make ads that grab their customers' attention, thereby increasing leads and keeping their audience engaged.

What is Instagram?

To put it simply, Instagram is nothing but a mobile application that helps people share their pictures and videos. It is a social networking platform that allows people to take videos and pictures and upload it on the web. People can choose to display it to the world or to a select few. The design interface of Instagram is extremely appealing with photos appearing in traditional Polaroid frames. The app allows people to use filters for their pictures, therefore making it visually appealing.

Apart from serving as a base for people to share their pictures, Instagram also helps brands reach out to their customers. It makes for a great platform to not only keep in touch with current customers, but also new ones. Brands use the platform to creatively display their products and enthrall their audiences. It helps to expand their creative space and draw more attention to their products.

The app is simple to use and is clutter-free, therefore making it the right platform to push captivating content that will appeal to the masses.

How Popular is it?

Instagram is extremely popular. According to reports, the use of mobile phones and mobile apps has taken over the use of any other type of social media in the US. Instagram is the most preferred app when it comes to sharing photos, and has over one billion active users in 2018, with numbers adding on every month.

Instagram has grown from strength to strength and come a long way since its launch in 2010. It had about 200 million users in 2014, which steadily rose to over 600 million in 2017. Today, almost every other person you know is on Instagram posting pictures and interacting with their favorite brands.

The app is available in 25 languages, therefore making it universal. Out of the one billion users, 60% of the people are from outside the US. This means that brands have global audiences and no person is too far to reach.

Instagram as a platform can be extremely entertaining with over 60 million photos uploaded every day. Of these, about 25 million are business images meant to serve as ads for brands.

Audiences can be glued to the platform for several minutes per day with an estimate of over fifteen minutes per day. Most of them are teenagers who actively check out photos on the platform throughout the day. In fact, about 75% of the users happen to be teenagers. This gives brands the chance to reach out to the younger audiences who can be a lot more interactive.

With more than 2 billion 'likes' and over 20 million comments a day, the platform provides brands with just the right level of user engagement. It is essential to have the right type of marketing strategy in place to ensure that audiences are not only engaged, but also keep them coming back for more.

Chapter Fourteen

Getting Started on

Instagram

Instagram is a platform that is easy to use owing to the simple interface it provides to users. It can be accessed via any device as long as there is Internet connectivity and a suitable browser that can open the site. The app is most popular as it is easy to access and upload pictures and videos just with the click of a button.

The app is available in the iOS and Android stores and will work well with any phone or tablet that supports these.

In order to get started with Instagram, the first thing to do is register with it. To create the account, the user has to choose a username that is unique and not already taken by another user. The next step is to set the password. For companies, it is best to use your name so that people can easily find and tag you.

The next step is to fill out personal details, such as the display name, addresses, gender, and email etc. Again, the company details have to be filled in.

The next step is to add a profile picture. It will be important to choose an eye-catching picture that is sure to appeal to the audience. Make it bright and bold and settle for your company's logo, as it will be easier for people to identify you. This picture can be changed easily at any time.

Next up, you have to write a bio or a description for your profile. There is a limit of 150 characters for this and can be left empty if you want, but it is best to describe yourself so that customers know what you are all about and whether or not they would like to follow you. Make sure you write an impressive bio.

The next step is to add in a website or other social media links so that people can connect with you on other platforms. This is a very important feature for companies as it will be easier to keep in touch with audiences. All they have to do is click on the link and people will be redirected. This helps to promote your business effortlessly.

All your posts can be made public so that it is easier for audiences to view your content, but there is also an option for you to make it private if you wish to limit your audience base, although this can go against you if you wish to capture newer audiences. If you have made it public, then anyone can start following you. If it is a private account, then they will have to send you a request that has to be approved in order for them to follow you.

Notifications

It is up to you to choose how you wish to be notified of the activities that take place on your account. Notifications can pop up if you are using the app but, if you are using it directly, then push notifications will be available for the activity. You can go to the app's settings to turn off the notifications if you like.

You can know what the new notification is just by the look of the bubble. A heart bubble stands for a like, while a speech bubble stands for a comment. There will also be a separate bubble when you are tagged in pictures and a new follower bubble when someone starts following you.

You will also be notified when you have a new follower on your page.

Connecting With the World

The main idea behind signing up in Instagram is to connect with people from around the world. Instagram provides you with the right platform to link your other profiles together, including Facebook, Twitter, and YouTube etc. You simply have to go to the sharing section to access these features. You can automatically share the same posts on the linked profiles.

The privacy settings featured on Instagram will extend to your other profiles on the linked accounts.

Posting Media

Anything you wish to post on Instagram has to be in photo or video format. The basic idea is to use these to promote the products. The photos and videos have to be of good quality to ensure that people recognize your products and can view them clearly.

Uploading Process

The second you turn on the app, it gives you the option of either uploading a photo or video taken from your camera, or choose something that already exists on your device. All you have to do is tap the button and the app will give you access to the camera where you can shoot a picture or video that will automatically upload. You have the choice to upload three-second videos that can be extended to 60 seconds. You must keep your finger on the record button for as long as you wish to record the video, and then take it off as soon as you are done recording. You can always record in segments and make a stop-motion video.

In order to post photos and videos that are already on your device, all you have to do is swipe left to go to the storage and access the camera roll. You can choose the pictures and videos that exist there to upload them. You can go to the specific folder to find the pictures you wish to upload by going through the drop-down menu.

It is best to go for photos and videos that are cropped into squares in order to upload as otherwise you will have to crop them. It is therefore best to take pictures that can be easily uploaded.

Attractive Pictures

You have the choice to upload photos and videos as they are or can choose to modify them to your liking. For this, you can choose filters that can make the picture look attractive and eye-catching, but be careful as it is easy to get carried away and end up using too many filters that can make the product stop looking like the real deal. It will be best to edit the content as little as possible to keep it original.

Instagram gives you amazing filters that can help you enhance your photo's quality. It can help to set a unique vibe and add a touch of vibrancy. Try out all the filters before choosing the best one. If you do not like a filter, then you can easily change it. You have the option to make it lighter or deeper. There are also basic features, such as rotating and flipping the pictures, adjusting the brightness, contrast, warmth, saturation, highlights, fade, vignette, and sharpening etc. etc. It will be best not to use these if you are not an expert or do not have experience in photo editing, as they can end up modifying the picture quality and making it look like nothing it actually is. One feature that is heavily used is the Lux effect that enhances photo quality instantly.

Instagram Filters

There are a lot of filters available on Instagram that can modify the way your pictures look. The whole idea is to make it as appealing as possible for the audience. Not only can they enhance the way pictures look, but also focus on the important bits of the product. For this, you can go through the list of filters available and choose one that best fits your needs. Each filter has its own set of attributes and they are discussed below:

- Normal is the option that lets you keep the original picture without any filters.

- The lo-fi filter uses enhanced warmth in the picture and a higher degree of saturation. This helps to draw out the shadows and make the colors appear richer.

- Earlybird adds warmth and a tint to the pictures that reminds one of old-world photos.

- Amaro is a filter that enhances the light at the center of the picture and deepens the focus.

- Rise adds a soft light and a glow to the picture and is one of the most commonly used filters.

- Inkwell is a filter that lets your colored picture turn into black and white.

- Sutro is a filter that lets you highlight and add shadow to the edges to achieve a burnt-out look and the purples and browns become more visible.

- Mayfair is a filter that has a vignette effect on the edge and turns the center into a glowing patch with a higher level of brightness. The entire picture will have a pinkish overlay and black borders all around.

- Sierra is a filter that enhances the whole photograph and leads to a fading effect; thus, providing a softer glow.

- Valencia is an effect that increases the exposure levels and warmth in the picture to give a unique touch. It can leave an antique look behind.

- Nashville gives you a nostalgic feeling with a pinkish tint and high temperature and exposure that makes it look bright and interesting.

- Toaster offers a vignette effect on the edges and a burnt effect in the center.

- Perpetua gives a pastel look to the picture.

- X-pro adds a touch of vibrancy and contrast and a golden tinge with vignette borders, thus making the picture look unique.

- Cream gives the picture a creamy look by modifying the warmth.

- Walden gives it an enhanced exposure and a subtle tinge.

- Aden gives it a bluish-green tinge that adds a degree of visible tint.

- Slumber is a filter that adds a black and blue hue to parts of the picture and drops the saturation level.

- Ludwig adds more background light and less saturation to the prominent parts of the filter.

These are some of the most commonly used filters in

Instagram and sure to be a hit with you. There are many more available to choose from and you can go with whatever suits your needs the best. Make sure you don't add too many at once and stick with a few that are best.

Sharing Photos and Videos

Once the photos have been edited using the chosen filter, you can share it on your screen. Instagram will allow you to add a caption to the photo or video. It will be important to make use of hashtags as they can get you noticed. Be liberal with the hashtags to make sure everybody can see it and find you. If you want to mention another account or brand, then they can be tagged too. All you have to do is use the "@" to tag them. Tap on the image that you wish to tag and then mention their username.

If you want to show viewers your location, tap on the location feature. This will tell your audience where you are based out of and will find it easier to track you. This feature is available when you are just uploading the picture.

Instagram Direct

This feature was introduced to the app and comes with a video feature. You can share images to certain users, which cannot be viewed by others. Direct messaging is a feature that allows you to send the customers direct messages. This is a very useful feature if you wish to collaborate with someone. It is also a great feature to reach out to specific customers.

Chapter Fifteen

Best Practices for Viral

Instagram Posts

As you know, Instagram is now much more than just an app that people use to share their photos and videos. It has become a place where brands promote their products and fulfill their marketing and business agendas. Instagram is not a platform that sells goods, but rather, plays hosts to brands who wish to sell their products.

Right from small companies to big companies, everybody can make use of the app's features to showcase and promote their products. It helps them reach out to customers who are scattered all over the world.

Instagram boomed when online shopping gained popularity, as it was easier for them to get people to see images of the products and add it to their carts. They could reach out to people on the other side of the globe without worrying about them having to walk into stores.

If you wish to use Instagram to promote your products and make the posts go viral, then there are some things you have to do, which are highlighted below:

- To start off, make sure your account is visible and has all the right details that will help people find you, so, right from your username to the logo to the pictures, everything has to be spot on if you want your audience to find you easily. Fill in crisp and clear information that will make it easy for them to find you and look you up.

- The posts you put out have to cater to what your audience is expecting of you. Viral posts work well if they meet customer demands and keep them entertained. You have to be able to generate interest in the post by incorporating things that are considered interesting by your audience.

- When you wish to promote your products, they have to be captured in a way that makes them look desirable. If your picture is mediocre despite the product being amazing, then it will not work well for you. People will share the picture if it is appealing and not because they like using the product, so make it vibrant and eye-catching if you want customers to go for your product.

- The product has to be photographed in a crisp

and creative way such that it appeals to the audience. If you have used Instagram and shared products on your page, then you will know that it is the beauty of the product or the way in which the product has been displayed that will make you share it. Try to take multiple pictures from different angles and make sure the background is clear and crisp. The camera has to be good quality and the lens has to be sharp. Go for a high-resolution camera to take high-quality pictures.

- Your products have to showcase or display an aesthetic appeal in order for people to like it. Arrange the products in such a way that makes people instantly like what they see. It should not be too cluttered and there should not be too many things on the page. It should be about the product and how appealing it can look to the audience.

- Consistency in your pictures will be important. The audience will expect consistency so that they can connect one picture with another. Work on coming up with themes for the pictures. They should be aware of the kind of pictures that are put out so that they feel motivated to follow you, like and share your images.

- If you wish to have your posts go viral, then

you will need a large audience. As you know, not all who follow you will like your posts. There will only be a few who will religiously like and share your products. You have to work towards keeping them and getting them to like your posts so that you push chances of making your posts go viral. We will look at ways in which to increase your audience base in a future chapter of this book.

- Do not limit yourself to just pictures, and consider putting out videos too. Videos can serve as much better promotion tools as they will hold your audience's attention for longer. If you have a YouTube channel, then you will find it easier to share the videos.

- Consistency is key. It is important to post photos and videos at consistent intervals. The audience should know when the next post is coming so that they are prepared to like the post. Mention it or make it known to them that you will be posting something at a certain time and keep them on the edge of their seats. Notice when people are active on the platform so that you can post the updates on time, every time, and push chances of amassing likes.

- A viral picture has to be well made. We looked at the filters that Instagram provides and can enhance your picture quality, but make sure you use other software that can provide you with quality editing tools that can make the picture look amazing. Right from adjusting the lighting to the sharpness to the brightness, make sure you give the photo a good look.

- A good way to get people to like your posts is by being customer-centric. This means that you post pictures by making customers the hero. It will motivate others to start posting pics with your products on their pages, therefore pushing chances of getting more likes.

- A good way to connect better with the audience will be by posting candid pictures taken in your company. It can help to create a good impression on your customers.

- Lastly, remember to stick with what works for you. If a particular picture has a lot of 'likes,' then stick with the same concept so that the audience can connect with it better.

Chapter Sixteen

Best Practices in Using Instagram for Marketing

As you know by now, it is important to use Instagram as a platform to promote products and reach out to a bigger audience. It is about being in the right place at the right time.

As you know, the new age is extremely sharp and will want to have things their way, so right from photos to videos to strategies, they will want to see things that appeal to them. This means that marketing agencies have to step it up in order to create a good impression.

Brands have to make use of Instagram's full potential as an advertising platform. It should be used for more than merely keeping in touch with customers and used to promote the products effectively.

Why is Instagram Important for Marketing?

Instagram has set itself apart from other social media platforms as customers can communicate and connect with others and brands of their choice. This means that brands no longer have to rely on traditional methods to communicate messages to their audiences. They can be directly involved with them and show them visuals of products that they are sure to fall for.

The platform gives companies the chance to showcase products creatively, such that it appeals to the audience at a deeper level. They will be able to connect with the story being told and want to be a part of it. Unlike old-school advertising where the pitch mattered, Instagram allows brands to take out language markers and put out pictures that are easy to connect with.

This means that the content that is put out will connect with the audience on an emotional level and there will be no language markers that will prevent them from understanding what the product is all about.

Since the app is easily available to everybody around the world, brands can have easy access to their customers. More and more have now started appreciated being in direct contact with the brands they love so that it is easier to not only look at products that are new and have just come in, but also be able to buy what they see faster.

83% of humans learning things come via visual aids. This means that people will be able to retain what they see for longer as compared to what they read; thus, it is important for brands to ensure that they put out the right images for people to see and know what is on offer for them to push chances of selling out products faster.

About 44% of Instagram's users prefer to be in direct contact with brands that make use of quality pictures of their products as it helps them to connect with the brand on a deeper level. Just one powerful picture can replace a thousand words and thus, it makes the advertising company's job much easier to have an engaging connection with the audience. The app helps companies to integrate their various social media platforms so that the audience can connect with each other.

Once aspect about Instagram that makes it so powerful is that it is cheap and affordable and anyone can use it to market products. Marketing agencies do not have to worry about shelling out a bomb to be able to advertise their products. All they have to do is sign up and start posting the content to get people to see their products.

The platform can serve as the primary source of information about all the products that are being advertised.

Creating Good Content

As you know, marketing is all about creating content that is informative and effective. The audience has to be able to connect with it and feel motivated to go for the products. Photos and videos that are unique and appealing can help to draw in the audience's attention, so care must be taken to supply content that is not only appealing, but also informative.

Competition will be rife, as more and more companies will be using the platform to promote their products. In such a case, it will be important to go for campaigns that will help you stand out. The audience has to feel like that and have to consistently keep coming back for more.

The content and pictures used have to showcase a story for the audience to connect with. There should be a genuine story that can help the audience connect with the products in a better way. It should be inspirational so that it is easy to sell your ideas and products to your customers.

As mentioned before, there are many filters to choose from to make a campaign stand out. Apart from filters, you must also engage them with concepts that they can connect with. For example, big brands use concepts such as greatness, endurance, and strength etc. and showcase celebrities or athletes doing their every day jobs while sporting the brand's products.

Benefits of Using Instagram for Marketing

As you know, Instagram can be used not just to share photos and videos, but also advertise products. Here are some key benefits associated with using Instagram to promote products:

- Customers love to have a visual reminder of the products to help them decide whether or not they would like to buy it. This means that the company has to put out pictures that will appeal to customers. Instagram therefore provides an easy platform for them to supply photos that will appeal to the audience, and also links to the products where it can be purchased.

- Instagram gives you a platform to tease customers by giving them a glimpse of the product that will be launched.

- What makes Instagram effective is the fact that it is free of cost for the companies to use and advertise their products. Marketing agencies do not have to indulge in paying up for advertising and use the same money to hire creative people who can come up with creative ads.

- Instagram makes it easy for businesses to keep in touch with customers and vice versa. It helps to remove a barrier that can exist between the two. This will lead to loyal customers who prefer to be in direct contact with brands so that it is easier to not only get information about products they like, but also sort out issues.

- You can always take the help of other Instagrammers and established people who can help you promote your brand. It can help to redirect more traffic towards your own page.

Social Media Marketing Importance

As you know, Instagram provides a very important outlet for companies to market their products and services. Here are some of the reasons why you should adopt it as part of your marketing strategy.

Instagram is All about Storytelling

Customers love to hear stories, be it about the brand they love, the celebrities associated with it or how their products are made. They will tune in just to get an insight into these things and to connect with the company in a better way. Instagram helps you to tell your audience stories that they can connect with and understand what goes on behind the scenes.

By sharing visual content such as photos and gifs with the audience, it will be easier for you to connect with them. As you know, the marketing ideology should always be product centric and thus, you have to ensure that you put focus on the products by making them a key part of the stories. The story should be able to push the product forward and get customers to embrace it. Connect the different aspects of the products together and create an interesting story.

Visual Content is Key in Marketing Strategy

Photos are one of the most fun and easiest ways to engage the audience. As per studies, photos produce a whopping 650% more interest in marketing strategies as compared to text alone. Thus, Instagram can provide a great platform to push products using photos as a background. It can be used to understand what your audience is looking for and use the same to push products forward. Work on the way the pictures are presented and use themes that are relevant and true to your brand's image.

Reach More People

It is easier to reach out to a bigger audience by using Instagram. The platform has millions of users who tune in every day to look at pictures and videos that have been shared by their favorite brands. Make sure you make complete use of the hashtag feature so that it is easier to not only find you but also make it simpler for the audience to access your products and campaigns. The hashtags have to be relevant and have a proper connection with your products if you want to sell it in a better way. It is also a good idea to come up with targeted ads that can be used to target a certain section of the audience.

Community Engagement

Instagram can provide the ideal platform to engage customers and has time and again beaten other social media platforms in terms of popularity including Facebook and Twitter. This shows us that Instagram is not only popular as a brand that can provide you with a platform to promote your brand among current customers but also get new ones on board.

Be an active part of the platform and comment and like your own posts. Be hands-on available for the customers and answer all queries that come your way. Use hashtags liberally so that it is easier for the customers to find your posts. Do not make it just about publishing photos and videos and get in there to connect with them better. Remember that just amazing photos will not be enough to engage the audience. You have to make sure their queries are answered and you provide them unique content that they can exclusively find on your Instagram page. Running contests can bring you closer to your customers and will be easier to engage them.

Feedback

As is with any social media platform, the marketing team can use Instagram to get the audience's feedback on products and services and also the marketing campaigns. Employ an effective team of members who can go through the different comments that are being posted on the page and products. They will tell you what the audience thinks about your products and the marketing campaigns. These comments can be used as a base to modify the products and the campaigns to make them more effective. Get your audience to engage in the conversations as much as possible and tag their posts when they use your products. Get them to tag you when they use the products or services so that you can enhance customer engagement. An app called Iconosquare will give you access to whatever fans are sharing about you so that you can know what is being said about you and assess the feedback.

Analyze Competition

As you know, Instagram has been around for almost eight years now and is an important marketing tool for many brands. You can easily keep an eye on your competition and know what they have been up to. Understand the marketing strategies that they are adopting and how it is working for them. Channel the best of their strategies so that your marketing team can adopt it.

Chapter Seventeen

Keys for Running an

Instagram Page

When it comes to successfully running your Instagram page, it will be important to resort to strategies that are unique to you. In this chapter, we will look at the things that can help you come up with a clear narrative to organize and run your page in a way that is not only appealing to your audience, but also easy to maintain.

The strategies can help you maintain a clean page that aligns with your company's vision:

- The first and most basic strategy is to go for a simple promise but deliver a message that is sophisticated.

- Be unique and different.

- Create a story using core concepts.

- Pick the right tools for the story.

- Associate stories that are accurate.

Let us look at each aspect in detail.

Simple Promise and Message

The brands that are currently doing well on Instagram are the brands that are using a simple promise and message. Instagram helps them to deliver quality photos and videos that their followers will like because of the simplicity and strong message they put forth. This strategy can be built based on customer insight and brand perception. The company has to know what the audience is expecting in order to deliver it to them.

The promise that is made should help the customer connect with the brand in a better way. It should capture the audience's attention and set up a deep bond with them. It is important to remember that the attempt should be natural and unique and not forced. The audience should be able to connect with it properly.

Successful brands are able to tell stories that are appealing and helps the audience connect with the products. It is an important aspect of marketing and best to employ skilled advertisers who know what to do. The story will have a bigger impact on the customer only if it is conveyed correctly.

Be Unique and Different

Brands that use Instagram are often rewarded for being different and unique in their approach. Using high-quality content that is different from what the audience is mostly exposed to will always help brands make a mark. Instagrammers like to follow brands that offer them variety and content that is engaging. It is therefore important for brands to come up with content that is unique and delivers on their promise by maintaining consistency and unique themes.

Create a Story Using Core Concepts

It is important to build up stories for the brand by using core concepts. They are as follows:

Authenticity

It is important to be authentic for the customer to be able to connect with you. As you know, audiences have become quite informative and can connect with many things to remain well-informed. This means they will have access to a lot of information so, if they see the same campaign elsewhere and find that you are repeating it, they might not like it.

The product has to be showed how it is instead of showing it as being different and more appealing. It can upset the customer after receiving the product if it is any different from what it is being shown as, so keep it genuine and authentic for the audience to like it.

Sensations

It is important to provide images and pictures that will create a sensory medium for the audiences to connect with. It should be able to help the audience make connections to their memories, and sensations etc. The images should engage their senses to create an engaging story. It should play out like a movie in their minds. It should be able to stimulate the various sensors, including smell, taste and touch through mere imagery. For example, if you are a restaurant that sells cupcakes, then the cake should be shown realistically such that people can imagine the smell, taste and texture just by looking at the picture.

Relevancy

Relevancy is key. The audience has to connect with the core concept that is being used as a base for the ads. It has to be relevant and make an impact on the audience. For example, Dove uses unique models for their campaigns in a bid to cover the various types of beauties that can exist in the world. It was all about breaking the stereotype and connecting with your audience.

Choose a Theme

Theme is an important aspect when it comes to building a story for a product. The theme will help to connect many different aspects and bring the story together. It will be important to identify the precursors of the theme and involve them in every picture you put up so that there is relevancy.

Your customers have to be told a story that will leave a permanent impression on their minds. If the stories are told consistently over a period of time, it will register with them in a better way. There will be depth and relevancy. It will help to turn to archetypes, such as freedom and strength, to create a story. People will be able to connect with such themes.

A personal narrative can always work in your favor. Customers will look at knowing what has helped someone and how. They will be drawn to the product if there are parallels between them and the storyteller.

Understand Storytelling

In order to come up with the ideal story, it is important for the marketing team to have a clear understanding of the different elements that go into storytelling. They have to know routes to take and use storytelling as a concept that revolves around beliefs and theories. Variety is key and what sells stories best.

Chapter Eighteen

Instagram Ads and Ad

Budget

When it comes to creating ads for Instagram, it is important to use the right tools to create appealing ads. Here are some types of ads you can choose to make for your products:

Photo Ads

Single image ads help to create about six ads that contain an image each.

- To create them, start by choosing the images you wish to use in the ads.

- Go through the library and upload pictures or choose free stock images.

- Add the caption you would want to use for the ad in the text field.

- The caption can be 300 characters long with the third line having ellipsis that will make the audience click on expand to view it fully.

- It is ideal to choose 125 characters for ads as otherwise it can be burdening.

- You can add a website link or a URL.

- You do not have to fill out all the fields such as the display link, headline, link description etc.

- Go to advanced options to change pixels or advanced tracking.

Video Ads

Single video ads are comprised of a video or a gif.

- To create them, go to the video thumbnail and add a video from your gallery or shoot one.

- Upload one that runs for 15 seconds for best results.

- If you wish to caption the video, then use an SRT file.

- It is best to add captions using 125 characters just as in the case of photo ads. Again, limit it to

125 characters.

Slideshow Ads

Slideshow ads are nothing but video ads that play on loop and can have 10 images with music supplementing it.

- To create them, go to the library and create a slideshow using the creator.

- Add the images and then arrange them to your liking and adjust the settings. Add in music if you like by choosing the icon on the top right.

Carousel Ads

Carousel ads are made up of images and videos.

- To make them, create cards for the ads. You can add up to 10 cards at a time.

- Add in headline or caption or text to each of the cards.

- You can choose to leave the description empty or add a URL.

- Add lead forms as it makes for an important step of the process.

- Regardless of the ad format you choose, create your lead form.

- If you already have one, then you can use the same or make a new one for the ads.

- If you wish to make one, then the fields to fill out includes the welcome screen, headline, image, layout, button text, questions, privacy policy, and thank you screen etc.

- A website link can also be added.

- Once done, click on the finish button.

- Once you click on it, you will not be able to edit it.

How Much Does it Cost?

How much the ads will cost will depend on the budget you set for it and whether you wish to use the manual or automatic bidding system.

As per marketing experts, running your ads on Instagram will be almost twice as cost-effective as running them on other social media platforms such as Facebook.

Although it is difficult to assess how much an ad can cost, it is safe to assume that the ad can be around $5. This is half of what it takes to come up with Facebook ads that can be around $10.

Don't worry about your budget going bust, as you will hardly ever over-shoot it when making Instagram ads.

Make sure you are well aware of what will be going into making the ads to be able to come up with an effective budget for it.

Chapter Nineteen

Using Instagram Live

Why Use Instagram Live for Business?

Just like you would use stories, it is important to use Instagram Live for your business. Not only can it be a great channel for connecting with your audience and increasing followers, but also going after business goals and generating leads. It can also help you get discovered better on Instagram.

Just like Instagram stories, making interesting Instagram Live videos can help you show up on the explore page that can make it easier to find you. It will be easier to broadcast your message and connect better with your audiences.

Instagram Live can be quite flexible as you get to decide what to broadcast and offer workshops, and answer questions etc.

You can make it fun and engaging for your audience to hold their attention.

How to Use Instagram Live for Business

Just like stories, Instagram Live can be used as an easy tool to broadcast a live video. Here are some things to keep in mind:

Viewers

You get to choose who to broadcast live to. You do not have to do it for all, and select only a few to broadcast to. You can choose to hide it from specific accounts by selecting the "Hide Story From" option.

ModeratingComments

As you know, when you go live, you allow people to comment on your video and you will not have control over what they say. If you wish to avoid any language that is inappropriate, then it is best to go to the settings and find "Comments" and go to "Hide Inappropriate Comments" and turn it from off to on. You can add custom keywords that you wish to appear in the comments.

Setting up a Live Broadcast

- Start by swiping right on the home screen or the camera icon on the top left to access the camera.

- Choose the "Live" camera option and "Start Live Video" option. If your notifications are off, then your audience might not be notified when you go live so make sure you switch on notifications.

- The number of people viewing will appear on the top and their comments at the bottom.

- Once done, touch the "End" button in the top right corner and "End Live Video.

Chapter Twenty

Instagram Analytics

Analytics play a very important role when it comes to understanding the effectiveness of the content that is being sent out. It helps the company understand the reach and the engagement. It is therefore important to understand the different performance indicators that can help companies know the effectiveness of their ad campaigns being carried out on Instagram.

Reach

Reach refers to the number of people who can view the content that has been posted on the brand's page. This content has to be relevant and great for it to be popular on the platform's search tab in order to reach a bigger audience. If you go by benchmarks, then it will be easy to improve the content that is being sent out. It helps to build content that appeal to the audience and increases brand value. If the profile has a lot of views, it will be easy to draw in more people to follow the page and increase the product's reach.

Engagement

Customer engagement is an important part of using Instagram as a means to connect with the audience. It can be measured through the 'likes' and comments that have been posted for a picture. The comments usually include the brand's hashtag, which will help to understand the activity taking place. It is possible to track down a lot of information, such as the filters that are popular, the content that is selling best, and styles that are a hit etc. It will be best to carry out a trial and error to understand what is working well for your audience and use it as a benchmark to improve the content that is being put out on your page.

Here is a summary of what analytics can do for you:

- Reach out to more customers and keep them engaged.

- Measure the key performance indicators.

- Create a benchmark for customers.

- Collect and understand the data.

- Make changes and improvements in the posts with the data that is connected.

Chapter Twenty-One

Introduction to Twitter

If you still haven't started using Twitter to promote your business, then you are surely missing out on a lot.

It is a potent platform that can connect you with your customers and enhance your business potential through several folds. It is vital for a business to be present on Twitter to make the most of the platform's reach.

It is no longer just a place for celebs to reach out to fans. It is much more, and a key outlet for any marketing agencies advertising campaigns.

As you know, markets are moving focus from outbound marketing to inbound marketing and thus, Twitter can play a very important role in helping companies do so.

Despite starting out humbly, Twitter has managed to capture the imagination of the entire world with millions of active users and new members added every day. Not only will you be able to keep in touch with ordinary people, but also in direct connection with celebrities.

If you want to make the most of your advertising

campaigns and reach out to your core audiences, then you have come to the right place! In the following chapters, we will look at the basics of Twitter and how you can use it to enhance your business.

Chapter Twenty-Two

Setting up a Twitter Page

Before getting started with Twitter, you have to know about a few things that can get you going. They are discussed in this chapter.

Choosing the Twitter Handle

The Twitter handle refers to your username or the identity on Twitter. It is the name that will get you recognized on the platform. It is a good idea to use your company's name when choosing a handle. Many individuals find it tough to have their own name on Twitter as it can sometimes be taken by others. It will be rare that someone else would be using your company's name as their handle; however, here are some tips to bear in mind while choosing your handle:

- If you are a business, then choose a username that is the same as your business name as people will be able to find and tag you easily.

- If the name is taken, consider adding a descriptor or an adjective to it to see if that will work out. It will make the name quite unique.

- Many companies like to make their handle look like their email address. This is especially important if a lot of your customers or leads are on your mailing list. They will be able to find and tag you easily.

- It is best to not use a complicated handle or just one element of the company's name, as people will not know whether you are a genuine brand. It will be best to use the name in entirety so that people can connect with you easily. Go for a simple, easy and fun handle that people don't just find easily, but will also feel like tagging more.

- When setting up the bio of the account, include the name of any one of the main people in charge of running the handle.

- It will be a good idea to use keywords in the handle. This will put you high on the search list in Google. That will make it easier for people to find you and tag you based on optimization by Google results.

- It is best not to go for a controversial name that might raise eyebrows. It might seem like a good trick to grab people's attention, but it might deter people from tweeting to you. It is best to have a decent handle in place. You might not be able to move your customers to a new handle and thus, it is best to choose the best handle and stick with it.

- Keep the handle short and concise. As you are aware, Twitter comes with a 140 characters limit, so people might be discouraged to tweet if the handle is long and they are left with lesser room to tweet the message.

Customizing Your Twitter Profile

A Twitter profile is the main page that people will see when they visit your Twitter page. It can be accessed by clicking on your handle or searching for you in the search tab. The interface is quite simple and is like Facebook's wall.

It will be important to have an attractive profile so that people are engaged and will click on the follow button. You have to create a good first impression so that it is easier to gain followers and hold on to the current ones. It has to reflect your personality and show the audience what you are all about and the kind of promotions they can expect on the page. Here are some tips to make your page look good:

- Ensure that you upload an image or avatar so

that it is easy to identify you. The image can be that of your business logo as people will be able to identify you easily looking at the logo.

- It is important to go for a background image or color that suits your business persona.

- Add a bio on the page that describes your business well. It should not be any longer than 160 characters.

- Share your website's link and other important information that you would like people to know about.

- It is easy to edit the bio and other aspects of the page by accessing the settings tab.

Twitter Features

As you are aware, Twitter can provide you with a lot of benefits that can help to take your business to new heights. If you wish to make the most of Twitter then here are some things to understand that can help you make the most of your Twitter account.

Word Limit

Twitter comes with 140 words limit. Many companies tend to still complain about it without knowing its full benefit. The limit can help to come up with a crisp and concise message that is to the point. Simply add in some great SEO words and you are good to go. Not only will it help you show up on top of Google searches, but also make it easier for people to find exactly what they are looking for. Adding a URL can also work as it will make people click on it.

Multimedia

It is a good idea to add multimedia to your tweets. It will help your audience connect better with the tweet. A video, GIF or pictures can all help them understand the message you are trying to send out. It will generate great interest among the audience. It is possible to link your Instagram and Flickr accounts to help them connect better. Twitter Live can help you stream videos live and directly engage with fans.

Embedding

Embedding allows you to embed your Twitter button on your website, email, and messages etc. It will get more people to click on it and increase your audience base. All you have to do is embed it on the page and ask people to follow you. It is also a good idea to mention about it on any packing material you use for your products to remind people about your Twitter page.

Integrating Your Twitter Account with Your Website

If you have a business website, then it will be important to integrate your Twitter handle page and vice versa. It should be easy for people to find and follow you.

To start with, simply embed the page on your website. It should be easily visible to your customers so that they can easily click on it. Have a reminder in place such as "Don't forget to follow us on Twitter!" so that it makes them click on the button and start following you.

The more the number of unique clicks, the more followers you will get.

If you have a blog post, then mention your Twitter account every now and then to get people to follow you. Sprinkle links to your page all over so that people can simply click on it and be redirected to the page.

Integrating With Other Social Media Accounts

Just as in the case of integrating it into your website, it will be important to integrate it with other social media accounts. Right from Facebook to Instagram to other platforms, it will be essential to link your Twitter page as it can help customers check out your page.

All you have to do is embed or add the URL of your page in your Facebook bio so people will click on it and be redirected. Again, do not forget to tell them they must check out your page.

It is also possible to embed Instagram pictures on your Twitter page and mention Twitter handle on your Instagram page. It is also possible to share select pictures. Simply copy the link of the picture you wish to share and add it to the Twitter page so that people can be redirected to the page.

Exporting Tweets and Automating

It is possible to export tweets, download them or take them offline. It will be important to do so for some companies who are trying to come up with unique and interesting campaigns. It can be taken offline and embedded in marketing strategies.

The easiest way to export tweets is by using external apps. Many apps can be downloaded and used to export or take the tweets offline. Simply download and install the app and run it along with your Twitter account. It is important to automate the account which means tweets can be automatically sent out.

This is a handy feature when you have to cater to a large audience and have only a few people managing the handle.

Automatic tweets will shoot off standard replies to queries. Say, for example, someone wants to know the price of a particular item and uses your hashtag; the server will shoot off the price that has been fed in by you and answer the query without you having to personally reply to it.

Some good apps to try out include Hootsuite, Social Oomph and Twaiter. They all have unique and distinct features that set them apart and can help you maintain an up-to-date handle. It is possible to schedule tweets and translate them and add in RSS feeds etc.

If you wish to maintain an interesting Twitter page, then hire a marketing team that is good at their job. It should consist of individuals who are experts and will be able to maintain a clean and neat page that is easy to access and clean to understand. If you do not want to hire full-time employees, then look up freelancers who will do the job for you.

Chapter Twenty-Three

Why Use Twitter for

Marketing?

As you know, Twitter can prove to be a great platform to not just help you connect with your audiences, but also carry out marketing campaigns that cater to the new age.

Businesses use it as a tool to promote their campaigns and gain an advantage over companies who do not use the platform for their campaigns. It is possible to reach out to many more customers who are scattered all over the world and increase brand loyalty.

It has been several years now since Twitter has been used as a marketing platform and will be essential for both big and small businesses to consider getting on the platform to promote their business. Even if you do not have extensive knowledge about Twitter, it will still be important to have a page for your business if you wish to promote it.

Here are ten reasons that will make you get your business on Twitter today:

Customer Connections

It is vital to connect with your customers. As you know, customers are the backbone of your business. It is important to use social media platforms to connect with them. Twitter is the second most preferred platform after Facebook and thus, you have to ensure that you make your presence felt. With more and more people joining daily and an average person spending at least ten minutes on Twitter; it becomes easy for brands to promote themselves and their products. Gone are the days when people went straight to their emails as soon as they woke up. They go straight to FB and Twitter to know what is happening in the world around them. Not only will customers be in direct contact with you and be able to buy the products easily, but also raise complaints that can be solved easily.

Branding

Branding is a quintessential part of any company's marketing strategy. Without proper branding, it will be difficult to reach out to customers. It is not only about big companies branding themselves, it is also about small companies who want to be noticed and recognized by customers just through visual cues. The best way to do so is by making your presence felt on

Twitter. If your company is brand new and nobody knows about it, then you have to tweet religiously and put out relevant tweets that capture your audience's attention. Some people go for a personal account first just to tweet about the company before launching the company on Twitter. This can work in your favor, as more people will start following the company's handle.

Customer Feedback

Customer feedback forms an important aspect of any business strategy. As you know, competition is rife these days, making it important for companies to be a notch above their competitors in order to make the most of their products. There should be room for constant improvement so that they can market their products and services if it specifically caters to the audience's needs. For this, feedback will be important. Customers can tweet their experiences with the product so that you know what they think about it. The tweets will be redirected to you and you can take their feedback into account to modify the product to their liking.

Marketing

Twitter is a prime tool to use to market your brand and products. Not only is it free, but it also comes with a big reach. All you have to do is assemble a dedicated team that can manage your handle. You can move your audience from your other social media accounts, such as Facebook and Instagram, to your Twitter page. With more and more brands resorting to using Twitter to carry out their campaigns, it will be important for you to get on it as well so that you are not left behind.

Updates

Twitter can be used as a means to provide updates about products. As mentioned earlier, customers will love to give you their feedback about products. Based on it, you will make certain improvements to your products. This has to be communicated so that it pleases them. The best way to broadcast it will be by mentioning it in your tweets. You can also specifically tag the person who has asked for the improvements so that they know you have worked on the product for them and have improved it to their liking.

Promotions and Contests

A trick that most companies use to get more customers on board is host contests or give out promo codes. These codes will let customers get a discount for their products. This will get more people to check your page out and follow you to access discount codes. You can get existing customers to retweet for you so that the message reaches a bigger audience. These techniques are adopted to garner more attention from potential customers. You can also have contests on your page. These contests will lead to better customer engagement. They will keep visiting the page for contests. Some ideas for contests can be coming up with a tagline for a product, or photographing the product etc. Make sure you announce competitions regularly to have your audience glued in.

Keeping an Eye on Competition

It will be important to keep an eye on your competition and the strategies they are adopting. It will also give you an insight into the kind of customers they have, and what they are tweeting to keep them hooked. All you have to do is go to their page by searching for them in the search tab. You will know what they are tweeting and also what they think about their competition. If you happen to find that there are communication issues between them and their customers, then you can learn from it and tweet solutions to them and win over their customers.

Going Viral

Twitter is a very popular platform to make things go viral. Right from posts to pictures to videos, it is possible to make many different things go viral, so, as soon as you have a good following, you can start writing tweets that can go viral. Making tweets go viral is a very popular strategy that many brands employ. Your team has to come up with a post that can set off a viral effect and get you noticed more. Using SEO words will make it easier to go viral and trending topics have to be incorporated in your tweets as much as possible.

Boost Sales

Use Twitter to boost your company's sales. It will help to increase profitability. Many popular companies have increased their business potential through several folds just by being on Twitter. It is especially beneficial to have an active account during spending season to make the most of it. This includes holidays and Christmas time when there will be a lot of traffic on the page.

Brand Loyalty

Twitter can help to enhance brand loyalty. It is one of the most important things that brands should care about. If you have loyal customers, then they will keep coming for more. They will also bring others along thus increasing your customer base. Using Twitter can help you engage with loyal customers and increase the number of people who will talk about your brand.

As you can see, there are plenty of reasons that make Twitter a great place for brands to showcase themselves and enhance their reach. You too can get these benefits if you use the platform for promotions!

Social Media Marketing Importance

Assess Competition

Twitter can provide a lot of information about businesses and their customers. Marketing teams use Twitter to understand what their competitors are up to and the strategies they are employing. Based on their findings, they will be able to come up with strategies that address the issues the competitors might face. Thus, Twitter provides a platform to assess and understand what people like and dislike and can plan marketing strategies accordingly.

Networking

Companies use Twitter to send and receive messages and can instantly connect with others. It is easier to network as Twitter provides the ideal platform to find like-minded customers and collaborators who can help to increase your leads. You can publicly address them or send them a direct message.

Twitter can prove to be a good source for relevant news. If you are looking for information that is not available anywhere else, then chances are you will find it on Twitter. You can go to the specific company's handle and scroll through the content to find what you are looking for. A good idea will be to follow the specific handles so that it is easy to remain updated on relevant and niche information.

Brand Building

Twitter makes for a good platform to build up your brand. It can promote brand awareness and expose customers, both new and old, to your brand's marketing strategies. The marketing team can post tweets on products and provide information about it. As mentioned earlier, Twitter is mostly used as a tool to provide information that is not available anywhere else. This will help brands build up a reputation and make it easier to reach out to customers the right way.

Website Promotion

Twitter offers a great platform to network with millions of people. This provides a huge base for companies to connect with customers and promote their websites. Be it regular customers or corporate customers, it will be easy to find the right audience to tweet to. Right from information based on the website to retweeting other important tweets, it is easier to reach out to the right people and expose them to your website. They will be redirected to it if you provide them with a link. Increasing traffic on your website can prove to be a great way to increase your leads.

But it is important not to tweet direct promotional messages or advertising messages on Twitter. It can prove to be too burdensome for some customers, especially if you have not engaged them in any other way. It will only work if you have been engaging them and built a close rapport with them.

The same extends to collaborators and other companies you are following.

Customer service

As soon as a new product or service is launched, you can tweet about it and get customers to ask you questions about the same. This will open up a line of communication with them and allow you to answer questions regarding the product. Come up with specific hashtags that can help you address the questions and find them easily.

It will be a good idea to set up a help desk on the platform that can consist of people who are good at giving short and apt replies to customer queries. Not only will it be easier to address the queries but also economical and a handy tool when the website is down. Your website might be down owing to heavy traffic and thus, the Twitter help desk can come to your rescue and answer any relevant queries.

Twitter offers companies with better search functions and allows customers to engage in thought searches on their accounts. This means, it will allow customers to see what others are thinking about specific topics. Say someone is looking for information about a particular lipstick. They will want to know what others are thinking about it and their thoughts and reviews. This is unlike Google search results where customers will only have access to niche topics and not be able to find any specific information. Thus, Twitter can give you what big search engines such as Google and Yahoo cannot and thus proves to be an important platform to use as part of marketing strategies.

Twitter searches are often optimized for various niches. It is often enabled for people to perform specific searches that cater to their specific needs. For example, if a customer is looking for a review of a specific handbag then typing that in can give them access to information that is specific to that handbag and filter out all other irrelevant information. This means searches are optimized based on niche keywords that are relevant to the products.

Chapter Twenty-Four

Best Practices for

Improving Loyalty and

Viral Twitter Posts

As you know, Twitter is a social media platform that brands use to promote their products and services. It makes it easier for brands to come into contact with customers and vice versa.

Brands can make use of this connection to influence their customers and get them to retweet, but it is easier said than done as customers will only retweet what they think deserves to go on their wall so it will be important to curate tweets that can appeal to the larger audience.

It is important to come up with tweets that customers will find attractive so polish your tweeting skills if you wish to get your customers to retweet for you. As per studies, majority customers admit to have bought products they saw on social media, such as Twitter and Instagram. This means Twitter can provide you with a lot of power to market your products and will be amplified if the posts go viral.

There are three main things to bear in mind when you wish to make a tweet go viral and they are:

- Write eye-catching tweets

- Get the timing right

- Test and measure the tweets

Write Eye-Catching Tweets

The very first thing to do is to write eye-catching tweets that will appeal to your customers. Here are some ideas:

Having Conversations

It will be a good idea to have conversations with your customers via Twitter. It will be like talking with them on the phone. Customers will have to connect with you at a deeper level. For this, the conversations have to be crisp and cohesive. They should make the customers feel inclined to buy the product. It should also make them recommend it to others.

- To win over loyalty, it is best to talk directly to

your customers. Reply to each of them directly. It will be important to reply to both negative and positive posts. If you end up not replying to the negative posts then they will think you are being careless or showing an attitude. It will be essential to reply to tweets as soon as possible so that you can get the conversation going with them.

- Put some thought into the tweets before putting it out. Think of it from your audience's perspective. Is it catchy enough? Will it appeal to all? Is there enough information in it? Is there enough humor to it? Answering these questions can help you come up with interesting tweets. You will know the kind of audience you are dealing with, and what will be expected of you.

- One mistake that companies make while addressing their customers is not knowing the difference between voice and tone. When addressing customers, the voice should be the same, but the tone has to be changed according to the situation. If there is a complaint that needs to be addressed, then the tone has to be understated so that it is easier to speak to the customer. Do not be defensive as it can anger customers and you might end up losing them.

- Make sure your tweets are professional and not

too casual. There should be a fine balance between the two. Have an engaging tweet ready for times when the traffic is at a maximum so that it is easier to hold your audience's attention.

Viral Expressions

If you wish to make your tweet go viral, then it has to convey the right message to the audience. This is possible through retweets where people will be able to share what you are saying with their followers. As per statistics, most of a brand's lead comes from retweets, so it will be extremely important for you to tweet something that is sure to get retweeted by a majority of your customers.

The best way to do so is to work on the kind of words and phrases that you will be using to tweet with. Here is a look at some things to include in your tweet:

- Make use of superlatives in the tweet, such as "awesome" "outstanding" and "brilliant" etc.

- Use words that will make customers take action, such as "see" and "look" etc.

- If you wish to explain a process, then choose phrases such as "how-to."

- Making use of visual words such as videos, GIFs and photos can be quite helpful in sending across the message effectively and getting them to retweet it.

- Include the audience in the tweets as much as possible. Use phrases such as "you tell me" or "let's do this" so that customers feel like you are directly having conversations with them.

It is seen that tweets that specifically asked for words to be retweeted were more popular. This means, all you have to do after tweeting is ask your audience to retweet it and a majority will do so. Simple things like "RT if you find these shoes lovely" will work.

It is also known that tweets that contain a large number of verbs and adverbs are clicked more often compared to the ones that have more nouns and adjectives.

Formatting

Work on your tweet's format and change it according to what the audience is looking for. Different marketing outcomes can be achieved simply by changing the format of the tweet. If you are looking for a direct response from your audience, then simplify the tweets.

Start with compelling words and phrases. Try to include

call-for-actions and use @ and hashtags to get people to notice your tweets. Look at popular tweets that have a lot of retweets and emulate the same, but make sure you keep your tweets original and stick with whatever will appeal to your specific audience.

Hashtags

Hashtags are a very important part of Twitter. Here are things to bear in mind:

- The hashtag has to be short as a long one can be cumbersome and annoying.

- The hashtag has to be easy to recognize so that people can easily use it.

- The hashtag should be easy to type and have simple letters.

- If you wish to use a hashtag that is already popular, make sure it has some relevance to you and your company.

The number of hashtags that are used in the tweet are also of relevance. Remember that you have to use hashtags at all times if you wish to be noticed.

Chapter Twenty-Five

Twitter Analytics

Twitter analytics can prove to be a boon for a business, as it will help them understand what is working well. Right from the marketing strategy to the kind of tweets that are being retweeted etc., there are many things that Twitter analytics can provide to customers. All you have to do is click on the "tweets" tab to gain access to the impressions, engagements and other such statistical data that can help you understand how your tweets are doing, and whether or not they are working for your brand.

You can also install specific apps that will tell you, or give you, an in-depth analysis of how your tweets are faring. Analytics are also designed to give you a timeline of new tweets that are moving through your site.

Most business houses use analytics to understand their audiences better; thus, clicking on the "followers" tab will help you assess their interests, what they are looking for, and their average ages etc. It will also tell you whether you have gained audiences or lost them and the timeline when they moved away.

It is easy to check how your ads are faring, and the

money that has been spent is well worth it. It will be easy to track the money being spent and how it is paying off; thus,Google Analytics can help you enhance your reach and engagement. It will tell you a lot about your customers and how to improve your tweets.

Chapter Twenty-Six

How to Set Up a Pinterest

Account

How many of you have a Pinboard set up in their office? Isn't it a great way to pin your family pictures, a recent holiday, or a place you would like to visit in the near future? The only problem is that your pinboard can only be viewed by you – is there any fun in that? Wouldn't you like to share your pins with the people you know and double the fun? That's where Pinterest comes in. As per the Pinterest website, Pinterest allows you to "organize and share all the beautiful things you find on the web."

Now, why would one use a virtual pinboard? The obvious reasons include image collection to help you plan a vacation, a wedding, or a family gathering and so on. That said, it's actually the social component of Pinterest, which can turn this activity into a growing network for business purposes.

So, how exactly does one set up a Pinterest account?

Getting Started

Unlike in the past, Pinterest is now ditching the invite-only approach and is open for everyone to join. It only takes about a few seconds to set up your account. Before you start with the sign-up procedure, you need to choose two different names, one that acts as your username, and the second one that is your account name. The name that appears on the top of your Pinterest page is your account name. If you are trying to set up a business account, visit the 'Pinterest for Business Account,' and click on the "Join as Business" tab. From there on, you can simply fill in your business details and complete the sign-up process.

Choose a Good Profile Picture

Your profile picture doesn't have to be a work of art, but you certainly need a picture that grabs attention, something that represents who you are, and is quite a standout in Pinterest. Let's be honest, regardless of whether you are setting up a personal or business account, your profile picture is going to make a significant impact on how people will view you, so don't hesitate to put in some efforts to click a great profile picture and edit it before uploading. For a business account, company logos in fresh and solid colors can be quite impactful on Pinterest's all-white background.

Make a Profile That Captures Your Business

Pinterest focuses on content creation – a platform where people are always on the lookout for content worth watching and sharing. This is exactly where innovative people are going to be hanging out as a way to grow their business. It goes for a personal account. People would like to get a view of your personal taste and talent, so it only makes sense to create a content-centric profile. Here's how that works:

- You are an organic chef and you pin an image of organically cooked dishes.

- My friend who is already looking to add some organic dishes to his diet follows your "organic dishes" board, sees the picture, likes it, and repins it to her "organic food" board.

- A lover of all things organic, not currently a customer, or ready to try out organic food yet, sees the picture, repins it to his or hers "all things organic" board. This person is now curious about who you are and what you do, so he clicks on to your profile page.

How do you wish to be seen? What would you like to tell people about yourself and your tastes? How can you help them get access to the things they love?

Use Pinterest Tools

Having the right tools for the job can be a key ingredient in your success. Luckily, there are a couple of tools that Pinterest offers for free.

Install the Pin to Your Browser

Pinterest allows free integration with the other online browsers on the Internet which can let you pin your favorite content to the page straight from the website. The "pin it" button is designed to only curate content, but also helps in linking your content directly to the website the content is sourced from.

Download the App

Regardless of whether you use Android or an iPhone,

you can easily download the Pinterest app to manage your page while on the go.

Use the Inbuilt Tools of Pinterest

You can look for Pinterest analytics features by logging on to analaytics.pinterest.com, or you can simply click on the Analytics tab located on the top of your profile page. Analytics helps in tracking the progress of your profile, people who are engaging in your pins, and the type of pins people are using from the website.

Create Boards

I would suggest creating at least three boards with some pins of each of them. If you were using Pinterest for business purposes, you would be better off not telling people that you are on Pinterest until you are actually on it.

Boards about Your Hobbies

This one is for people who are using Pinterest to connect with other like-minded individuals. Keep this board full of fun-filled pictures, and allow others to lighten up. The beauty of using Pinterest is that you can showcase your talents, passions, or business and have some fun while you do it.

Boards Designs to Help

Don't be too promotional on Pinterest. If you are marketing your own brand of clothes or food, come up with something that can provide some valuable information to the viewers.

Boards Regarding Your Products or Services

Boards like these can be a great way to promote your business. Be subtle when you are trying to promote your products, or when you are just starting off. You want to come off as authentic as possible.

Use the Right Keywords and Tell Your Network

Be strategic about the titles you use for your pin boards. For most people, Pinterest acts like a visual search engine to find the services they are looking for, so ensure that your pins top the search results associated with the keywords you use. Secondly, use your network to spread the word about your Pinterest boards. You can use other social media platforms like Twitter and Facebook and ask people to find you on Pinterest.

Keep Pinning

Now that you have set up your profile, keep pinning, and don't stop in your tracks. The more you continue to pin, the more creative you will get. If you are a beginner, you need to be patient with yourself, and allow some time to pass before you start getting followers. Continue exploring even when you don't get any comments, 'likes' or repins. It's all a game of consistency and connection. Try your best to come up with innovative content every other week, remember to engage with your audience, and, before you know it, your profile will be the one that others look for guidance on how to get started.

Chapter Twenty-Seven

Use Pinterest to Drive

Traffic to Your Blog

Do you wish to drive more traffic to your blog? Pinterest could be your key to get a good return on investment (ROI). Pinterest is becoming increasingly popular as a site that people can use to read articles they like, but how do you use it?

Create a Blog Board

Creating a personalized blog board for your blog articles makes it easy for your followers to stumble upon your blog posts as well as follow them. The title of your Pinterest blog board should be the same as the blog page title. For instance, if you sell jewelry on Etsy store, and your blog is about DIY projects, then name the Pinterest blog board the same as the website blog name you would use like "My Etsy" or "DIR crafts."

When you write your blog post, don't forget to pin it on the blog board. Be sure to include:

- A link that takes you to your blog article.

- An image that represents your post.

- A short summary or a quote from your article.

Create Boards That Are Related to Lifestyle

You probably already have several boards on the business Pinterest account but, if you don't, then you need to start creating your boards right now. Pin it using various content like lifestyle images, household tips, and much more associated to your blog theme.

When you pin blog articles in this manner, remember to include:

- A link that takes you to your blog article.

- An image that represents your post.

- A quote or summary of the article associated with your board theme.

You want to show how your blog article is in sync with the emotional, as well as personal, context of the board theme you are using.

Images

Pinterest is all about images. It may seem contradictory that you have to upload beautiful images on your Pinterest board, when all you really want is the viewers to read your content. Nevertheless, great visuals are a smart way to draw traffic to your website, increasing the possibility of followers actually reading your blog. Think of Pinterest like a glossy magazine that is fun to read. In order to capture the attention of the reader, your pins need to be a total visual treat.

Engage on Pinterest

Just like any social marketer would, you need to engage with your followers. The more you engage with people who follow you on Pinterest, the more they will want to connect to your blog, as well as other sites. There are a lot of ways to try to get to know your market better while on Pinterest. Here are a few tips:

- Pin original and relevant content.

- Pin consistently so your pins are often seen by your followers.

- Keep looking for follower's boards for better content ideas.

- Return the favor when someone follows you; follow them back.

- Ask questions asked in your blog.

- Repin, comment and even like your follower's pins.

Make it Easy to Find Your Blog Post Pins

Pins on Pinterest are indexed not only within the site, but also in search engines such as Google. Ensure that you are practicing smart SEO tricks when you pin your blog post on the site. The first thing you need to do is to ensure that your pins are extremely searchable. Don't forget to check your account settings, and ensure that your "search privacy" setting is edited to allow other public search engines to find you. Below are some SEO tips for Pinterest:

- Use significant keywords for your blog posts.

- Your blog title should be the same as your blog board title.

- Use keywords in the images you may upload.

- Include relevant hashtags.

Prepare a Contest Board

A smart way to drive some traffic to your blog post is to post something fun, interactive and engaging content on it. Run frequent contests straight on your blog, and later pin them on the contest specific board.

This is completely different from the "pin it to win it" contest. Contest-hosting is an amazing way to drive traffic to your website. Contests are not only fun, but they are also engaging, making it easier to drive traffic to your blog. You can also make a contest pinboard and later pin the blog hosted contest on it.

Feature Your Blog Writers

Generally, the more followers you have, the better they will be able to relate to you and vice-versa. This strategy works wonderfully well if you wish to develop blog traffic to your own blog. Allow the followers to know the face behind their favorite articles. Develop a fun, customized pinboard which showcases your blog writers.

This is what you should do when you pin to a blog writer's board:

- Include the face of the author.

- Write a quick bio, using a unique lifestyle-related hobby.

- Write a short quote from your blog post while attributing it to the author.

Include a "Pin it" Button on the Blog

When the blog articles are shared by your followers, their friends and followers are likely to read them too. It's a sort of mouth publicity for your blog. To do this, ensure that you have a "pin it" button on each of your blog posts. Make it as easy as possible for the pinning followers so they can share it on the websites they love the most.

As per Pinterest, the "pin it" buttons are capable of creating a significant rise in bringing the referral traffic back on to your website.

Use Article Pins

Article pins share more information as compared to the "pin it" button. As they are pinned, they include various pieces of information by default such as the story, headline, story link, and summary. These pins are very impactful in giving an incredible boost to your blog site. To add the Rich Pins to your website, you need to apply to Pinterest but, before you do, you need to have a blog site that meets the Rich Pin requirements.

Social Media Marketing Importance

Pinterest has been around for quite a while now and makes for an important social media-marketing tool. Here is why you should use it for your marketing strategies.

Enhance Brand Awareness

When you use a personalized Pinterest page that exclusively caters to your brand, then you will have the chance to show customers your brand's true identity and the values you swear by. If you have engaging content, then it is easier to connect with your customers and they will be more aware of what your brand truly represents.

Increase Traffic

The ultimate goal of using any social media platform is to increase your website's traffic. Each of the pins that are made will include a direct link to the website such that clicking on it will take the customer to the product's page. Thus, Pinterest can provide the ideal platform to find new customers for your products.

Increase Audience

Using Pinterest on a regular basis can help to keep the platform active and remain a big part of the marketing strategy. As and when people start sharing your pins, it will get more exposure with a worldwide audience looking at your company's pins.

Increasing Ranking

Pinterest works on the basis of keywords or SEO words. So, it is important to incorporate them as much as possible when you pin something on your board. It can help people find you easily. It will increase your rank and help you show up higher on Google searches.

Chapter Twenty-Eight

Best Pinterest Practices

In the world of social media platforms, there are certain mediums that go unnoticed, but then there are some highly interesting ones that easily appeal to the users. One such medium is Pinterest.

As per new research, Pinterest has become the 4th largest referral network, and these numbers beat Yahoo, while sitting just behind Google. This visual social networking niche that promises to drive a huge traffic for image-rich sites is becoming more popular day-by-day.

Below are some tips which can help you use Pinterest in a better fashion:

Plan

Make a content strategy that focuses on the lifestyle of your target viewers. Stay away from narcissistic displays on your blogs, and, by that I mean, you should not have the "me syndrome" and not focus on pinning only your products. You need to connect with your followers by trying to figure what is it that they aspire and would like to see on your board. If you consistently strive to offer value to the readers, you will easily establish a rapport with them.

Set Goals

Set your own goals. What are you looking to create? Brand awareness? Wish to drive traffic to your website? Or helping people with some life solutions? A good rule of thumb is to target 25% of all the website traffic from social media. This could include various social media platforms like Instagram, Facebook, and Twitter. Now it's for you to decide where Pinterest fits into the equation, and accordingly decide how you will track, and report.

Align

Your pinboard cannot be haphazard. You will have to put in some time to strategize how you wish to position your brand. Check out how competitive the market is with regards to your niche, and start aligning it with the timeliest, popular, and topical conversations. For instance, if you are running a boutique, pin the trendiest of clothes - Prom Dress (topical); New Year's Eve

Dresses (timely).

Optimize

Google totally loves Pinterest. Don't believe me? Try searching for some of the most popular topics and it will pull up images predominantly from Pinterest. All you must do is focus on keywords that are important for your brand, align them with your knowledge about audience searches, and incorporate them in your pin descriptions as well as board titles. Sounds too simple? It is, except that it may take you some time to figure the precise keywords if you are a beginner.

Engage

I can't stress this enough. Pinterest is an interactive community, which requires a two-way communication. You can't just keep receiving likes and comments from your followers without you reciprocating them. If you constantly lag on returning the favors of your readers, you will start losing the followership, for people want to relate to you, so try and engage as much as you can and as often as you can. Like, comment, or repin on boards and pins of others. Increased interaction with your followers can also translate into more traffic to your blog.

Organize

Sort out your boards. Organize it in a way that they seem fun but organized at the same time. Also, try to come up with fun names for your board. As much as keywords are important, it's equally important to have fun while doing so. You don't have to stick to the clichéd bunch of keywords that comes up in every Google search. Allow yourself to get creative with it. Lastly, ensure that you chose a board cover image to a pin that best represents the topic on that board.

Diversify

You don't have to stick to one niche if you like variety. In fact, it can be great if you experiment with different pins for different sets of audience. Pinterest allows you a good opportunity to connect with a wide variety of audience as per your interests. Take the leverage and create pins and boards, which cater to all segments of your consumer base.

Evaluate

Always track your success. What is it that's working for you? What pins and boards are people viewing the most? Which are the posts that are getting frequent "repins"? How effective is your pin board in driving traffic to your website? Are you close to your goal or do you need to change your strategy and work differently to accomplish your target? Keep asking yourself these questions in a way to evaluate yourself where you stand in relation to where you wish to be. Evaluate the bounce rate of KPIs to make sure that the traffic that is being driven to your site is directed to the appropriate place. Don't forget to leverage your ability for using specific links to track.

Enjoy

The most important thing to do when you are using Pinterest is to enjoy. Pinterest was created with the aim of allowing the users to have as much fun as they can while using it. Pinterest is a stunningly beautiful visual medium, and we should use it to the fullest. Encourage others from your social group to pin your content with some exciting scavenger hunts, some fun contests, and trivia, by using different hashtags.

Conclusion

Once again, I want to thank you for choosing my book and I hope you found it of some help. Social media marketing is here to stay, but setting up that campaign on your chosen platforms is only the first step. Once your community is defined and your presence is firmly established, it's up to you to keep your activities online at a long-term professional high standard.

You must constantly research your audience. You must determine when the best time is to post on your sites and, perhaps more importantly, what to post. You should make good use of tools that will help you track your performance, such as Google Analytics. Listen to feedback from your audience and make sure you are in constant touch with what's hot and what's not.

Now, all that you need to do is use all the information provided in this book to optimize the way you use social media.

All the best!

Made in the USA
Middletown, DE
23 January 2019